FEAR NO EVIL

Charles Hamlin

**Kneeling on the right
Sgt. Charles "Chuck" Hamlin
Ball Turret Gunner**

H.I.S. PUB G
The Publishing Group

www.hispubg.com
A division of HISpecialists, llc

Published by HIS Publishing Group, a Division of Human Improvement Specialists, llc
Contact: info@hispubg.com

Cover image provided by Bill Varnedoe, courtesy of Stars and Stripes

Title Page image provided by A. Kaye

Cover by Hadeon Design Studios
Edited by Libby York Stauder
Interior Design by Ryan Conway

Please refer to the Appendix for photo credits.

Library of Congress Control Number: 2011917450
ISBN: 9780615513652

Printed and bound in the United States of America

Dedication

Dedicated to the 28,000 airmen who sacrificed their lives for the cost of freedom during WWII.

ACKNOWLEDGEMENTS

We wish to thank the Mighty Eighth Air Force Museum in Pooler, Georgia, for the courtesy of their help and the photos they provided so generously.

We also wish to thank the 385th Bomb Group Historical Association for allowing us to use the actual accounts of missions flown by their crews, as well as to thank their president, Tom Gagnon, 814 Staffordshire, Sun City, Florida.

TABLE OF CONTENTS

FOREWARD

This book is about the U.S. 8th Army Air Corps from 1943 to May 1945—more specifically, it is about the incredible B-17 bombers and the brave men who flew them. It is an attempt to put the B-17 into its proper place in history—and to bestow upon it the esteem it so richly deserves from our country.

The B-17 comprised two-thirds of the United States bomber force, and the men of the 8th who flew them suffered catastrophic losses, in terms of percentages. The crews managed to complete only 27% of their assigned missions before being killed, wounded, taken prisoner or suffering some kind of breakdown.

Both the B-17s and the B-24s were equally responsible for the success of America's bombing campaign that played such a major part in the defeat of Germany. However, the B-24, which was one-third of the force, should be covered in a separate publication—one that can do justice to the noble aircraft and its crews.

These stories are true accounts of actual combat missions, as told by the crews that flew them while stationed at the 385th Bomb Group in Great Ashfield, England. (There are also some accounts of missions flown by other groups.) The missions flown were

Original sign hanging at the Great Ashfield Airdrome in England

from England to various parts of continental Europe. The primary target: Germany. Hearing from the men who were there will take you back in time so you can appreciate the great sacrifice they made for our current freedom.

Many of the accounts here illustrate the unique hardships the crews faced nearly every day. Imagine yourself, hit by flak or shot up by a fighter...wounded, trying to make your way to a hatch in a spinning, out-of-control airplane, only to bail out in temperatures of 30 degrees below zero, landing on top of a house, in a frozen river, or wherever...at risk of being killed by a pitchfork or, at best, becoming a prisoner for the next few years. Yes, these were some grim times.

You probably need to know a little more about our situation in 1941 and 1942 to appreciate stories of the air campaign in Europe and its great effect on the "big picture". By the end of 1941, Japan had bombed Pearl Harbor, wiping out half of our Pacific Fleet. Germany had conquered most of Europe and dealt England a crippling blow at Dunkirk by literally pushing some 200,000 British troops into the sea. England was so poorly equipped at that time they had to use private pleasure boats to rescue the survivors.

The air war in Europe was unlike any war in history in that it took place five miles above the earth. First, the elements had to be conquered, then the mission had to be flown and the bombs dropped accurately. Today we fly into space and think nothing of it. During WWII, there were no standards from which to operate; what was happening was a "first" and we knew very little about it.

While we were busy ramping up and trying to get ourselves organized, Germany was rapidly expanding its territory and tightening its grip on Europe. In many expert opinions, there were two major mistakes on Germany's part: the Russian campaign, with the tremendous pressure it put on the German army's western forces, and the failure to fully develop atomic weapons and other weapons such as a stealth fighter-bomber.

While rumors definitely circulated that the Germans were developing powerful weapons, we seemed to be totally unaware that Germany was in the final stages with weapons that could make a tremendous difference in the battle for Europe.

One of these weapons was a stealth fighter-bomber called the HO-229. Although it was an aircraft primarily made of wood, it could attain speeds exceeding 500 mph. Its twin jet engines allowed it to reach altitudes far above the capabilities of Allied aircraft, and its twin 30-mm cannons

HO-229 German Stealth Fighter-Bomber

were devastating weapons. The HO-229 was essentially a "flying wing", and was thought to be the forerunner of a larger model capable of crossing the Atlantic.

While building a wooden aircraft may seem amateurish and unimportant, one must remember that many aircraft have been made of wood over the years, including the British Mosquito and Howard Hughes' famous Spruce Goose. The Spruce Goose was an eight-engined monster with a 320-foot wingspan. This aircraft was test flown successfully in California in 1947.

Perhaps if the Germans had remained allied with Russia longer, it would have given them the time needed to perfect these weapons. These two turn of events were, of course, proven to be mistakes...by the valiant fight put up by the Russian people in defense of their homeland, and the tremendous and constant pounding of Germany's military targets and industrial complexes by both the United States Army Air Corps and the British Royal Air Force. Warnemunde and other sites that were active in atomic research were bombed many times during 1943 and 1944, as well as in 1945.

If Germany could have moved the clock back six months, many believe they would have succeeded in their ambitions for world domination. It is noteworthy to recognize the importance of "Operation Alsos", which was an effort by the U.S. government to determine the extent of the Germans nuclear energy project. They were able to seize nuclear resources, materials and personnel that were then used in America's own research. Operation Alsos was also commissioned to make sure the information didn't fall into the hands of the Soviets. Thus, it only took a few months for the United States to perfect and deliver the A-bomb once we had gained the full knowledge from the German scientists.

It is assumed that without the ferocious bombing and their problems on the Russian Front, the Germans would have perfected the A-bomb in close to the time it took the United States; that is, four to six months from the beginning of 1943. An A-bomb dropped on London in the middle of 1943 possibly could have settled the war in Germany's favor. We will never know for sure, but we do know that we prevented it with an all-out effort by the Royal Air Force and the Mighty Eighth.

Cover of LIFE Magazine featuring the Mighty 8th on July 26, 1943

B-17 "FLYING FORTRESS"

The first B-17 was built by Boeing Aircraft Company in 1930, and was initially flown in 1935. One look at the B-17 by Richard Williams of the *Seattle Times*, and it was aptly named the "Flying Fortress". The B-17 had a cruising range of 3,000 miles at 180 mph, and it could carry a bomb load of 6,000 pounds. Some 4,750 B-17s were lost due to enemy action during WWII; 17 B-17 airmen were awarded the Medal of Honor.

The B-17 flew at nearly maximum ceiling, which was 35,600 feet—an altitude where temperatures reached 40 degrees below zero. A 10-hour mission at 25,000 feet over Europe in winter, even on a "pleasure" trip, was unsavory at best. Throw in 50 or 60 German fighters armed with 20-mm cannons and several-hundred anti-aircraft guns and you had a very good chance for disaster.

B17 - Latest Rumor

When it came to the demands of war, America's airplanes were not yet completely ready for the job. The way a B-17 was designed, it was difficult for crew members to bail out in case of emergency. The pilot, co-pilot, engineer, navigator and nose gunner bailed out through a hatch in the bottom of the airplane right under the pilot's seat. The radio operator, two waist gunners and the ball turret gunner bailed out through the main door of the ship near the waist gunner positions. The tail gunner left via a small door near his position in the tail section of the aircraft. This sounds like a highly organized, very logical plan, but in a spinning airplane at 20,000 feet, with wounded aboard and all your oxygen gone, it's a little difficult to proceed logically.

The German anti-aircraft guns fired a shell, which burst when reaching the altitude of the aircraft they were firing at. This burst was called flak, a contraction of the German word for anti-aircraft gun, *Flugzeugabwehrkanone*, and it looked exactly like what it was—a small bomb exploding. Upon detonation, the shell

Flying Through Flak

fragmented into hundreds of pieces, each piece going in a different direction. It was not impossible for a single shell to destroy two aircraft if it exploded between them.

B-17s also were not heated to any normal degree, because the windows and hatches had to remain open for the gunners to fire their guns. Consequently, crew members wore bulky and uncomfortable clothing, which still didn't keep them warm. The dogs that Russia sent into space in 1960 were better equipped.

One of the stories you will read, "Another B-17 That Came Home", tells of a plane that limped back to base with the nose of the aircraft blown completely off. The story is far from believable, yet it is a compelling example of the hardships flight crews faced, and, like all the accounts herein, is completely true.

THE MISSION

FLAK TROUBLE

"*What'd you say, Dan? You want me to tell Ronnie he's going to die? How the hell am I supposed to do that? Ronnie doesn't even know what the hell's going on; he's been in the turret for six hours.*"

"*That's not what I said,*" Dan replied matter-of-factly. "*I said, establish some communication with him—shout, tap on the turret, or whatever. Find out if he's still alive and try to tell him what our problem is. Tell him we are doing all we can to get him out. Tell him to try to let us know how he is...is he injured? Does he have oxygen? Is his suit working?*"

Dan Harding was our pilot and Ronnie was our ball turret gunner. Dan's day had started normally for a mission day. It's still unclear exactly what happened. It kind of snowballed. First, the flak hit, then the hydraulics went out and we were unable to crank the gear down when we checked it. The oxygen stopped flowing and we had this problem with the turret. All this, plus having two crewmen hit by flak.

We were flying our B-17 back from a raid in Germany when we took a heavy hit from flak, knocking out our hydraulic and electrical systems, including our landing gear, brakes and ball turret controls. The turret controls were so badly damaged that we could not open the hatch. The turret was locked in the "guns up" position, leaving the hatch down and impossible to open. The 50-caliber machine guns in the ball turret rotated in every direction except up; they shot from the horizon down, and you could shoot at the ground and every direction up to the level of the aircraft. The ball turret protected the aircraft from fighters below or on the same level as the bomber.

Dan was forced to make a decision over whether to ditch in the channel or crash land, wheels up, at our base in England. If we ditched in the channel, the ball gunner would be killed on impact or drown in the turret. If we crash-landed, he would also die on impact because the turret would be sheared off the aircraft when it hit the ground.

When the flak hit, Dan let down to 10,000 feet immediately, a better altitude for many reasons, including "bail out", if necessary. He didn't know if the oxygen in the turret was out, or about the power, but he suspected both. What he did know was that the ball gunner was still alive because he was tapping on the turret after we reached 10,000 feet.

Dan also knew the interphone was out because he hadn't received any answers to the last three oxygen checks (each crew member must check in with the pilot at 10-minute intervals when at high altitude).

Things like this had happened before. They were situations where there were no winners; everybody lost and there was nothing to be done about it. As badly as the crew felt, they couldn't help Ronnie.

Every man on the crew had seen men die, and it never got any easier. Rumor had it that some men were so badly torn up by the flak that they could not be removed from their positions—they had to be washed out with a fire hose. The crew had to think about this all the way home and wonder if it would be Ronnie's fate. The silence only made it worse.

We eventually concluded that the ball gunner was doomed, if he wasn't already dead from the flak hit. The first hit could have knocked out his oxygen or his heated suit. Either of these would be fatal for him at such a high altitude. We were at 23,000 feet when the first burst hit. We had to think about the rest of the crew. Two of them were already wounded.

Dan's thoughts at the time included, "*What about my other nine men? If we ditch, they could all die; if we crash-land, most likely they will survive—damaged, but alive.*"

Ditching

Aside from exploding, being shot down, or crashing in enemy territory, ditching in the English Channel or the North Sea was the most feared ending a mission could have.

The North Sea is connected to the Bay of Biscay by way of the English Channel. All three are rough, cold, and unpredictable. It seems the weather is always bad; rain, wind and high seas are the norm for any season, and the temperature of the water is never far above freezing.

Aircraft ditching in these waters might have a 50/50 chance of survival. The British Air Sea Rescue Service did a wonderful job, but winds, fog, rough seas and bitter cold played their part. It was always a case of whether there was enough time to launch and complete a rescue.

This illustration, taken from the USAF "Pilot Training Manual for the B-17 Flying Fortress", relates instructions for ditching:

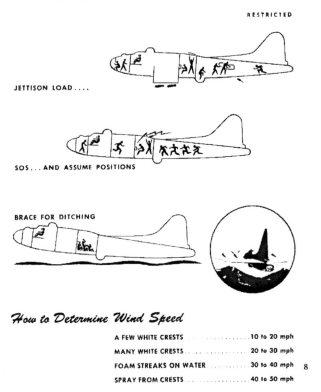

RESTRICTED

JETTISON LOAD....

SOS...AND ASSUME POSITIONS

BRACE FOR DITCHING

How to Determine Wind Speed

A FEW WHITE CRESTS	10 to 20 mph
MANY WHITE CRESTS	20 to 30 mph
FOAM STREAKS ON WATER	30 to 40 mph
SPRAY FROM CRESTS	40 to 50 mph

8

FLAK TROUBLE (CONTINUED)

As hard as our pilot's decision was, there was really no choice but to sacrifice the ball gunner to give the rest of the crew a chance. *"Well, at least most of the crew is okay,"* Dan thought grimly. *"Our main problem, at least for the time being, is the ball turret and the landing gear's hydraulic system. Maybe the engineer can fix it, but it doesn't look likely since part of the hydraulic line was torn open by the flak hit."*

The co-pilot was treating the waist gunners who had been hit by the flak. They both had leg wounds. One of them had been hit in the thigh, but it didn't look like any bones were broken. Still, he was bleeding the most, so the co-pilot took him first.

Billy, the left waist gunner was hit in the ankle and could not put any weight on it. The flak hit may have broken his ankle. The bleeding was stopped and the ankle wrapped tightly. Both gunners were calm and composed after having their wounds taken care of. Billy was a help trying to get the ball open, but to no avail. The turret wouldn't budge. The co-pilot signaled back to the tail section and got a thumbs-up from Ricky, the tail gunner. Thank God for that—it was Ricky's last mission.

Dan was accustomed to making tough decisions. His father was an alcoholic who blew most of his money on booze. He was completely unreliable and not at all concerned with the problems that confronted the family. As the oldest son, Dan was called on to participate in many of the family's issues and decisions. By sheer grit, Dan's mom helped him get through high school and one year of college before he enlisted in the U.S. Army and went to pilot training.

Dan scored big with his instructors in flight school. They were pleased with his common sense, quick thinking and high grades. He was a natural as a bomber pilot and was a "buddy" to his crew; they were his only concern. The welfare of his crew was most important to Dan, and they could do no wrong. They were one happy crew and out of respect to their skipper, they got together and christened the airplane "Dangerous Dan".

uring phase training, the crew Ronnie was on got stuck at Langley Field and broke up when the pilot chickened out, taking the job of operations officer at Langley. The rest of the men were reassigned to other crews that were short a member.

Ronnie went to the commanding officer (C.O.) and requested that he be put on the next crew that needed a radio operator. He told the C.O. that he wanted to go overseas as soon as possible. *"I don't suppose you would like to go as a ball turret gunner?"* the C.O. asked. *"I'd recommend you for the promotion to tech sergeant if you decide to go."* Ronnie's immediate answer: *"When do I leave?"*

The flight overseas was big stuff for a crew all under 22 years old. Here's Ronnie's account of the trip:

"We went from Langley to Mitchell Field in New York, where we got our special equipment: a 45-caliber automatic, a watch, sunglasses, a leather flight jacket...man, this is the big time. I really felt like a flyer.

The first leg of our travels, from Mitchell to West Palm Beach, was sort of a submarine hunt down the East Coast and good practice for our later Atlantic crossing from Belem, Brazil, to Morocco. While in Morocco, a few of us visited the medina (Moroccan bazaar)—not a good choice. We traveled by horse and buggy, and half-way back, our driver stopped, removed a wheel and demanded more money. What a ballsy move! We were all armed with .45s, but that didn't seem to impress our driver. I guess the son-of-a-bitch knew what he was doing because, in the end, we didn't shoot him...we paid up. The highlight of the trip was breakfast in Belem, which featured about 20 different types of bananas—some a foot long and others as small as a peanut.

After a couple of days in Morocco, our flight to "The Wash" in England seemed like it would be a welcome pleasure. The Wash was a small bay on the northeastern coast of England that served as a combination staging area and base where in-Theater crew training was done. It had classroom facilities as well as ground-to-air gunnery practice. We took a gunnery refresher course there before reporting to our group, but The Wash turned out to be a disaster. Terrible weather, awful food, and we were restricted to the base—great. Wished we saved some of those weird peanut bananas. The only redeeming factor at The Wash was an old English fisherman who brought clams. Might not seem like much, but it was a real treat for a kid from Maine. Odd how small things can become luxuries when you're away from home.

Arriving at our final destination in England, the 385ᵗʰ Bomb Group, we were in for some more training. The crew trained in local flying, slow timing our aircraft (flying at low speed to break in new engines), practice formation flying, and aircraft recognition, among other things. At this time we were issued our personal gear, assigned to a Nissen hut (pre-fabricated barracks) and met other crew members who had been there a while.

We were photographed and issued an "escape kit" (in the event of getting shot down over mainland Europe). The kit consisted of a pair of old shoes (the Germans could recognize an American by his shoes); a compass; German, Dutch, Belgian and French currency; a silk map that could be hidden in a very small place (like a cavity of any kind); and the photo they had taken (to give to the 'underground' so that they could get you an ID card in a hurry).

Hundreds of crewmen made it back to their bases with the crucial help of the underground resistance. Once a crewman made it back, it was forbidden for him to return to active mission flying. The Germans could consider him a spy if he showed up more than once, and they could execute him if they so desired. It was also against policy to allow an airman to continue flying combat once he had been shot down. The Germans, if they knew the crewman had been previously shot down, would torture him to reveal details about the underground that may have helped him escape. If they discovered the underground, it would mean death for the men and concentration camp for the women.

Our flyers were issued a .45-caliber automatic pistol before they left the States, but many of them did not take it on missions. The chances of survival were better if you didn't get into a gun battle with the enemy.

Also, the locals were more likely to kill you if you were armed. The huge number of Air Corps prisoners in Germany attests to these beliefs.

Next, we had a few very important questions for the veterans we had just met, like: Where's the action? How are the girls here and are there any available? Where do you go to get a good steak? What time do the pubs close? Is there any trading to be done with the pub owners or the girls? If there isn't, what am I going to do with all these damned chocolate bars?

To the crew, those were the most important questions to ask. No one thought of asking anything about the enemy—we would find that out soon enough. We were given a wealth of information, like where the nearest hole in the fence was, and we were told to forget about the town of Great Ashfield. If you had to go to town, go to Elmswell or to Ipswich, if time allows.

The best piece of advice we received was to save our money and strength for London, a soldier's dream come true."

"*I*'*m not even supposed to be here. Hell, I'm not even a ball gunner, I'm a technical sergeant, I'm Ronald Kramer. I'm supposed to be a radio operator, sitting in my nice roomy radio room observing radio silence, with my ass under a couple flak suits, throwing chaff (aluminum foil strips to confuse German radar) out the hatch for a living. I don't think our radio operator has ever fired a gun, and if he did, he'd probably hit one of our own ships.*

Why did they send me to radio school, freezing my ass off for three months in the middle of winter in Wisconsin, to observe radio silence? I could have learned how to throw out chaff in an hour! All I learned in radio school was Morse code and how to play ping pong.

What's wrong with the guys up there? Why aren't they cranking the turret up? It's not too comfy in here with that oil and hydraulic fluid leaking in.

I knew something would go wrong on this trip. The phony that flew this thing on the last mission sprung the damned hatch door, and now it won't close properly. Can't believe he didn't know you couldn't crank the turret up with the hatch open. Good thing the oil and the piss from the nose section freeze. Better than smelling it all the way back to the base. Oh, that smell—like spending eight hours in a Depression-era outhouse. Most people wouldn't have a clue what it might smell like, unless, of course, they had spent some time in an outhouse. The one redeeming factor is that at least it is only the commissioned officers doing the pissing. It wasn't like I was being pissed on by my entire crew."

Piss, by itself, has quite an acrid aroma when in a confined space, but when mixed with motor oil, hydraulic fluid and engine exhaust fumes, it becomes quite bearable. There are two things that tend to improve the odor: you know you have lost altitude because you are in a warmer climate, and if you have lost altitude, that means you are getting closer to home. That's good.

Flying in a ball turret is very different than being trapped in one. You can always climb out if you're just flying in one. When you're trapped, you can't even rotate the guns; you are on your back, looking in one direction only. The turret gets smaller and smaller and you are helpless. Another problem is that the ice you are breaking out of your oxygen mask constantly is freezing on the gun sight window, making it hard to see. Hell, a kraut could be flying formation with you and you wouldn't have a goddamn clue. It makes you wish you could pull into a gas station and get your windshield cleaned.

PICCADILLY

"*When was the last time I went to London?*" Ronnie thought, allowing his mind to wander. "*London's a blast, sitting in Lyon's Corner House, eating a black market steak and drinking that dollar-fifty-a-bottle scotch.*" Lyon's Corner House in Piccadilly Circus was the local hangout for London's "party girl" crowd. You could find any girl who wanted to meet men in the Corner House.

Many of the GIs who met a girl during the blackout, which was every night, discovered that they had picked up and negotiated (we referred to them as "deals") with a very ugly girl. You see, those "deals" were made outside during the blackout. The Corner House forbade girls to actively solicit us on the premises.

What was amazing was how the girls would arrive at a price that was exactly 10% of the customer's pay. They would run a hand down your sleeve where your badges, stripes, officer insignia, hash marks and flying status were, and could calculate how much you were paid. This all happened in about three seconds. This so-called "accounting show" alone was worth more than the rest of the whole experience. Of course, any self-respecting girl who felt the smooth sleeve of a private in the darkness would disappear into the night like a ghost.

As gracious as our British allies were, and they were most gracious, some things took getting accustomed to. One was the belief by many of the English girls that if you had sex standing up, you were less likely to get pregnant. Although our troops knew better and considered these beliefs not credible, they went along...reluctantly, of course, in order not to anger our hosts. The results of this activity took its toll on many of the trees surrounding the bases. Many of our soldiers swore they, unexplainable, grew an inch or more in height during their tours in Great Britain, due to these unusual activities.

The biggest question we were always asking, *"Why is it that when you meet a fabulous chick, she has a friend who looks like a hippo?"* The good-looking gals would always insist, *"I have a friend and I can only go out if we double date."* Of course, then you had the dilemma of where the hell would you find a guy to go out with the hippo? We would laugh, *"Is it the dish who uses the hippo for protection or is it the hippo using the dish for bait?"* To this day, I still don't know the answer to that question.

The airmen in England were not accustomed to, but really enjoyed, breakfast in bed that was cooked up by their companion's mother—a quaint but lovely custom. All this would be topped off by a rare hot shower, providing you had a shilling left to put in the "Geezer" (a coin-operated water heater that seldom worked).

When the sirens signaling an air raid went off, you could hear the airmen saying, *"An air raid—who the hell cares? I'm not about to waste a perfectly good 48-hour pass sitting in a worthless air raid shelter."* There were plenty of places open during the raids. In fact, there was this one little restaurant a few blocks from Piccadilly that served a good steak, even though it tasted suspiciously like horsemeat. We liked the restaurant because it was "L" shaped. For instance, if you were sitting in the front near the windows, you could always move to the back and take refuge behind the "L" when the air raid warning sounded. Of course, we all knew what the real air raid warning sounded like—a V-2 engine stopping. You knew damned well you had better get behind something solid, like the other part of the "L" in the restaurant, because the buzz bomb was on its way down.

THE ROUTINE

We woke up at 0400, scratched our balls for five minutes, took a shower, got dressed, and waited for the truck to pick us up. We ate chow: two real eggs, SOS, real bad coffee, and toast. Briefing was next, everyone waiting for the briefing officer to pull back the curtain and expose the target and the course to it and back. Sometimes, the course line went all the way across Germany and off the map. This, of course, was accompanied by a few loud groans of protest.

The briefing covered flak along the route, possible fighter problems from the *Luftwaffe*, weather, target details, secondary targets and escorts by our own fighters, if any. Then, off to pick up our gear, guns and heated suits, and off to our planes.

The mornings in England can be very cold in winter, but every "hardstand" (hard-surfaced areas where aircraft and vehicles are parked) had a barrel full of aviation gas burning to generate a little heat. That was when most of the rumors flew around. Someone always seemed to have a close friend on the general's staff who fed him the very latest on the tactics Headquarters was using. Then we would hear the "All aboard", which meant we would taxi out and wait for the green flare.

The fighter escorts in the 8th Air Corps were far beyond anything we have seen—before or since. These pilots went to any length to protect our bombers. It's impossible to describe the feeling that comes over you when you first spot your escorts. At first, you don't know if they are friend or foe...they appear to be just specks in the sky. There was a tremendous difference, though. Some of those "specks" were trying to kill you and some were going to protect you, even if it cost their own lives. Of course, you hoped those specks wouldn't be shooting at you. The escorts—P-51s, P-47s and P-38s—would hover, two- or three-thousand feet above us, ready to swoop down on anyone molesting the group.

Our first problem was getting off the ground, no easy job from a short runway with trees just after the end of it. Everyone sweats the take-off, but soon the sweat turns into fear...fear of trying to get into formation in overcast skies, with hundreds of other B-17s trying to do the same thing.

The overcast in Europe is much more of a problem than any place that comes to mind, sometimes lasting the entire mission in various forms. Climbing out through several thousand feet of overcast (with no radar) was a mid-air collision nightmare. Every group had collisions; ours had 12 of them, each one fatal to most of the crew.

The crew could breathe easy when they reached altitude over the channel, but this was short lived because the flak started when you reached the coast of mainland Europe. It seemed like the Germans knew every route we took and thoughtfully placed anti-aircraft guns along those routes.

German anti-aircraft guns were very frightening; they were large, powerful and accurate. For the most part, the Germans used their famous 88-mm guns, although they also used 105 millimeters. The 88 fired a shell measuring about three feet long and five inches in diameter. They could fire three rounds every 20 seconds. The projectile would ascend to your altitude and explode. The shrapnel, from the size of a dime to the size of a coffee cup, would come at you with more speed than a bullet. The blast was equivalent to having four hand grenades packaged together and exploding with each burst. It was said that Berlin was defended by 500 anti-aircraft guns, all manned by master sergeants.

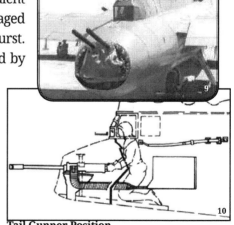

Tail Gunner Position

"This is not the flying they taught me," thought Dan. "Flying is what birds do. Taking off and guiding 30 tons of metal, gasoline and bombs is more like driving a truck on the Alaskan Highway, blindfolded and with no brakes."

The quarters were cramped, to say the least. The tail gunner is on his knees for eight to 10 hours.

Top Turret Gunner

The top turret gunner stands up in his turret for almost the entire mission.

And those were "roomy" areas compared to the ball turret. The ball turret gunner was in a ball measuring 44 inches in diameter, made of aluminum and Plexiglas, along with two 50-caliber machine guns, 1,100 rounds of ammo, a gun sight about the size of a shoebox, plus oxygen equipment.

He didn't even have room for a parachute, not that he would be able to bail out, anyway. It would take him about 10 minutes to get out of the ball and into the fuselage, get his chute on, make his way to a door, and finally throw himself out of the damned plane. This seldom happened, especially without the help of a waist gunner.

Ball gunners knew all too well that their chances of survival were very slim if the aircraft went down. Everyone knew that there were very few ball gunners in German prison camps. There just isn't time for them to bail out.

Ball gunners, in general, accepted this fact of life. All combat flying was voluntary; you could quit at any point, and many crew members did just that. The thought of flying these missions was petrifying.

In the infantry, you could dig a foxhole. In the armored division, you had a steel tank around you. In the navy, you had a huge ship. But in the air, you had up to 500 anti-aircraft guns firing at you and if a shell burst within a hundred yards of you, you'd most likely be hit.

"Ronnie never got a break," thought Dan. *"From the few stories he has told me, it didn't sound like he's had a very special life. I wonder how he's handling it."*

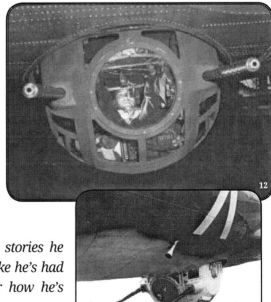

Ball Turret Gunner

THE LANDING

Ronnie Kramer was brought up in a little town in Maine. His dad was a boxer known as "Crash Kramer". Unfortunately, the most accurate part of his ring name was his crashing as he hit the canvas. A couple years of this crashing was enough for him, so he sold cars for a living. Ronnie had a high school sweetheart, but she met a shipyard worker after Ronnie joined up, and that was that.

Birthdays were hard for Ronnie to enjoy. He told us a story about his eighth birthday when he went to his father's garage. All excited, he reminded his father that it was his birthday. One of the customers tossed him a quarter, but his dad gave him nothing. He said, "Wasn't that great—my dad gives me nothing, but a stranger gives me a quarter."

In the plane, Ronnie was alone with his thoughts. *"My God, what am I doing here? What can I do? What will they do? Will they be able to crank me up? Will they ditch? How much fuel do we have left? There can't be much—we've been up here for at least eight hours. Why is it so cold in here? Has my suit shorted out? Should I fire all the ammo so it doesn't explode on landing? Maybe the flak hit the tires. How much damage has been done to the ship? We took quite a hit from that flak. Is anyone wounded? It's getting a little warmer...looks like we're at about 10,000 feet."*

Assuming the possibility that the ball gunner was still alive, Dan had taken the ship to 10,000 feet to eliminate the need for oxygen and to get out of the freezing weather. Use of a "walk-around" oxygen bottle was not required at this altitude, making it a lot easier to take care of the wounded and try fixing the damage to the ship.

Ronnie reasoned, *"The channel should be coming up any second now. Why are they beating on the turret? They must be having trouble getting me up. I wish I knew what was happening up there...I'll be okay when the gear comes down, but that might be an hour away. What if the gear won't come down? The turret won't move...maybe the gear won't come down, either. What about that plane in Pyote? They made a crash landing and everyone came out of it okay. Maybe I'll be lucky. What about that guy who rode the tail section down from 12,000 feet? He lived; maybe I have a chance. What would the world be like if I'm not in it? Who will do my stuff? I don't want to think about landing in here; I've too much stuff to do. I can't think of anything right now, but I have a lot of stuff to do.*

We must be around 2,000 feet now. We're close to the base. Why aren't the wheels down? Aren't they working? How about the hand crank? They need to get the wheels down. We can't make a wheels-up landing with me in here.

There's the base. There's the runway. We're making a straight-in approach. There must be someone wounded aboard or maybe we're out of fuel.

We can't do this! They're going to crush me! CHRIST, that's what he's doing! There's the meat wagon and the fire trucks. Jesus, are they waiting for me? I don't want to die. I'm too young to die. I need to see my mom. I love you, Mom, and you, too, Dad.

*The Lord is my shepherd...I shall **fear no evil, fear no evil, no evil**...*

How did I even get into this mess? What the hell did I do wrong? I just wanted to be a soldier, wear the uniform and pitch in to help my country. I knew there was a lot wrong with the government. It's definitely not a fair government. Congressmen "work" a few years and retire with full pay and privileges, including medical."

(The foot soldier retires with 20 years of service and gets 50% of the poverty wages they paid him while he served. Any officer retires at "highest rank held". Meanwhile, the grunts must be retired for 10 years before they get this "extra". The congressmen and all the other government workers should get their healthcare at the nearest Army hospital. Maybe then service would improve.)

Dan was on his radio, *"Hardlife Tower, this is 0088. Do you read?"*

"0088, Hardlife."

"Hardlife, 0088. Request permission for a straight-in approach and a wheels-up landing. I'm on final about 40 miles out on a heading of 340 degrees. I have wounded aboard and a mechanical problem. I need to speak with maintenance."

"0088, Hardlife. You are cleared straight-in, number one to land. What is the nature of your problem?"

"Hardlife, 0088. My gear is locked up, I have no hydraulics and my ball turret gunner is trapped inside the turret with no way out. I need to talk with maintenance for any possible solution. I am also low on fuel, but may have enough to go around if necessary."

"0088, Hardlife. This is Sergeant Elton, your crew chief. Have you tried the hand crank override for the gear and the turret?"

"0088. Roger that—nothing works."

"0088, Hardlife. Have you checked all fuses and breakers?"

"0088. Roger that."

"0088, Hardlife. Can you pry the ball up using some kind of lever, like a gun barrel or the like?"

"Roger that, Hardlife. Nothing works."

"Hardlife, 0088. I'm still on final. Shall I go around or land?"

"0088, Hardlife. You are advised by the group commander to go ahead and land. No solution has been found, and in consideration of your wounded and your fuel situation, you must land as soon as possible. I'm very sorry to say that no way has been found to raise the turret, either. You are ordered to make a straight-in, wheels-up landing on runway 34, number one. Emergency vehicles are in place. Our prayers are with you."

HARDLIFE STORIES

Heavenly Body

Told by Edwin Perry

Naming our airplanes was the sport of the day in the 8th Air Corps. One of the most famous was "Heavenly Body", named after a recent Hedy Lamarr film.

My cadet pilot training was with class 43K at Santa Ana, King City, Chico and Stockton—all in California. I completed B-17 transition at Roswell, New Mexico, in March 1944. Crew training was at the "Rattlesnake Bomber Base" at Pyote Army Air Field in Texas. (The fact was, there were a whole lot of rattlesnakes in the area; thus, the air field was appropriately named.) On leaving Roswell, I picked up the six sergeants assigned to my crew at Salt Lake City, Utah, and continued to Pyote. I was very fortunate to get this crew—they were all sincere and very professional. From Pyote, we headed to Kearney, Nebraska, where we were processed for overseas duty and issued a new B-17G, which we checked out and test-hopped. We flew through a rough night of thunderstorms to Bangor, Maine.

The next day we flew to Gander, Newfoundland. While waiting for favorable weather to cross the Atlantic, the four of us headed to the Officers' Club, where the subject of naming our airplane came up. Several names were kicked around and the name of a new movie, "Heavenly Body" starring Hedy Lamarr, surfaced. This name was a unanimous choice, so we composed a letter to Miss Lamarr, requesting permission to name our B-17 "Heavenly Body".

We then flew the Atlantic, landing in Prestwick, Scotland. We were taken to Stoke-on-Trent and on to Valley, Wales, where we were assigned to the 385th Bomb Group.

After flying a few missions, we were assigned a new B-17G model. At that time a package arrived, containing two beautiful pictures of Hedy Lamarr. The

Picture of Hedy Lamarr painted on the nose of "Heavenly Body"

8x10 glossies were autographed and accompanied by a letter from Hedy, saying she would be honored to have the plane named "Heavenly Body". We chose the picture of her in the big hat, and the group artist did a great job reproducing it on the nose of our plane, B-17G #44-6008. Our crew was split up for an orientation mission, with me flying co-pilot with another crew. Our first mission with crew intact was to Stuttgart, Germany, on the 16th of July, 1944.

Unfortunately on September 6, 1944, while we were living it up on a 48-hour pass in London, the Charles Lament crew flew "Heavenly Body" on a mission to Bremen, Germany. The aircraft took heavy damage and the pilot was forced to ditch into the English Channel. The pilot and co-pilot were killed, but seven other crew members survived and were rescued.

Our last mission was scheduled for October 30, 1944. We flew a total of 34 missions with the same crew. Thank God, no one was injured. For the record, we completed every mission that we started. I could not have had a more outstanding crew assigned to me.

Prior to every mission, our navigator, Fred, and the bombardier, John, would arrive at the aircraft in a weapons carrier and start lining the plane's nose with flak jackets. This made the nose a little more resistant to anti-aircraft fire. After several of these were aboard, I would confront Fred, *"That's enough—we'll never get this crate off the ground." "Just a couple more,"* was his reply.

Prior to each take-off, Fred would come up to the cockpit and hand me a slip of paper, reading: *"If we get extensive damage over the target, here's the heading to take."* Invariably, it was a course to a neutral country like Switzerland or Sweden.

On a mission to a secondary target in Coblenz, Germany, we were on the squadron leader's left wing. While turning on the initial point of impact (IP), the crew on his right wing inadvertently salvoed its bombs. The following crews also dropped their bombs on the IP and peeled off around the target. The crew on the right wing stayed with us and our three planes continued to the target—only two of them with bombs. Needless to say, with only three planes over the target, we took a terrific beating from flak. A shot came through the bottom of the fuselage and knocked out the entire instrument panel in front of Nick, my co-pilot, and me. I knew this had come close to the navigator station, if not through it. I got on the interphone, *"Fred, are you all right?"*

After what seemed like 10 minutes, but was more like 10 seconds, Fred came on, *"Yeah, I'm okay."* What a relief to hear his voice! The flak did splinter the left side of the navigation desk.

We were able to stay in formation back to the base and, on the wing of another B-17, we were able to make a successful let down, approach and landing with no instruments.

During another mission, Jake Jacobson, our tail gunner, called to me, *"Ed, they're tracking up our rear end."* I told Jake that we were on the bomb run in tight formation with little room to maneuver. Jake came back, *"Ed, they're getting closer—right on our tail."* Then, suddenly, Jake hollered, *"I'm hit, I'm hit!"*

I told Bob Brow, our waist gunner, to get an oxygen bottle and a first-aid kit and go back to help Jake. We dropped our bombs and cleared the target when I called Bob to find out how badly Jake was hurt. Bob came back laughing. Flak had come through the side of the fuselage and hit the 50-caliber ammo belt, knocking it against Jake's leg. He thought he had been shot. Jake never lived that one down.

Robert Glakeler was our ball turret gunner. At age 33, he was, by far, the oldest member of the crew, so his nickname was "Pappy". I told Pappy that he didn't have to stay in that fishbowl in the target area—no German fighters were going to hit us with all that flak around. Pappy said, *"I want to stay in the turret. I point those twin 50s straight down and spin around. If the flak gets too close, I shoot back at the ground."* Sadly, Pappy was killed on a B-26 mission in Korea.

A landmark event for the 385th Bomb Group was the 200-Mission Party (a celebration of the 200th mission the group had completed), held during the first week of October, 1944. The group stood down, with no missions for three days and a carnival set up in the middle of the runways.

General Jimmy Doolittle honored us with a visit. The Glenn Miller Band played for us at a dance in the hangar. To get some female dance partners, GI buses parked in the local towns with signs on the sides, inviting girls aboard for the big dance. There was no shortage of beautiful girls for the dance; they came in all sizes and varieties. It marked a great leap forward in the social lives of both the soldiers and the English population—all in all, a great success.

Unfortunately, Glenn was lost over the English Channel on his way to France the following December. It was December 15, 1944 and

Replica of Captain Glenn Miller's downed plane.

Captain Glenn Miller was on his way from Bedfordshire, England, to Paris, France, which had recently been liberated, to play a concert for the troops. He was flying in a U. S. Army UC-64, a single-engine passenger aircraft called a "Norseman". The airplane was reported missing over the channel and has, to this day remained "missing". No trace has ever been found. There have been several theories about what happened to Glenn, including an espionage theory and a friendly-fire theory, but the incident remains a mystery.

Captain Miller was 40 years old at the time of his death. He will be remembered as a great patriot, enlisting in the Army at age 38 so he could be a part of the war effort. The Glenn Miller Band still exists, playing for our military events, as well as for civilian occasions.

Captain Glenn Miller

Hedy Lamarr died in Orlando, Florida, on January 19, 2000 at the age of 86, probably without knowing her beautiful picture was painted on the nose of our plane. Many people don't know that Hedy was also an electronics inventor. In 1940, she invented a jamming device to block German radar; this was only one of her approximately 45 patents. After her patent expired, a major corporation adapted her device and now uses it to speed satellite communications around the world.

ANOTHER B-17 THAT CAME HOME

Told by 1st Lt. Lawrence M. DeLancey

After literally losing the nose of his B-17 Flying Fortress due to a direct hit by flak over Cologne, Germany, on October 15, 1944, 1st Lt. Lawrence M. DeLancey, 25, of Corvallis, Oregon, returned to England and landed the crew safely at his home base. Each man walked away from the plane, except Staff Sergeant George E. Abbott of Mt. Lebanon, Pennsylvania, who was killed instantly when the flak struck.

It was the combined skill of Lt. DeLancey and his navigator, 2nd Lt. Raymond J. LeDoux of Mt. Angel, Oregon, which enabled the plane and crew to return safely.

"Just after we dropped our bombs and started to turn away from the target", Lt. DeLancey explained, "a flak burst hit directly in the nose and blew practically the entire nose section to shreds. The hit obstructed my vision and that of my co-pilot, First Lieutenant Phillip H. Stahlman of Shippenville, Pennsylvania. What little there was left in front of me looked like a scrap heap. The wind was rushing through. Our feet were exposed to the open air at nearly 30,000 feet above the ground. The temperature was unbearable."

> "Just after we dropped our bombs and started to turn away from the target, a flak burst hit directly in the nose and blew practically the entire nose section to shreds."

"There we were, in a heavily defended flak area with no nose and practically no instruments. The instrument panel was bent toward me as a result of the impact. My altimeter and magnetic compass were about the only instruments still operating—and I couldn't depend on their accuracy too well. Naturally, I headed for home immediately. The hit that had killed Sergeant Abbott also knocked out Lieutenant LeDoux back in the catwalk (just below where I was sitting). Our oxygen system was knocked out, so I descended to a safe altitude. Lieutenant LeDoux, who had lost his instruments and maps in the nose, did a superb piece of navigating to even find England."

During the route home, the crippled aircraft encountered flak yet again, but due to evasive action by Lt. DeLancey they were able to return to friendly territory. Even without their nose section, without brakes (there was no hydraulic pressure left), and with obstructed

1st Lt. Lawrence DeLancey's crippled B-17

vision, Lt. DeLancey made a beautiful landing, to the complete amazement of all personnel on the ground at the field.

Other members of the crew included: Technical Sergeant Benjamin H. Ruckel from California, engineer and top turret gunner; Technical Sergeant Wendell A. Reed of Shelby, Michigan, radio operator gunner; Technical Sergeant Russell A. Lackman from Rockport, Massachusetts, waist gunner; Staff Sergeant Albert Albro of Antioch, California, ball turret gunner; and Staff Sergeant Herbert D. Guild from the Bronx, New York, tail gunner.

My Fourth Mission

By Rubin A. Stein

It was Easter Sunday in 1944 when I was awakened by Gat, our friendly "waker-upper". He advised that I, navigator on "Curley's Kids", was to fly with a crew from another squadron.

I was told to check in with Joe Hart, the pilot and aircraft commander of the "Spirit of Chicago". Meeting with the crew, a bunch of grizzled veterans who had made it through 25 missions, I sat through the mission briefing. The target was Warnemunde, a base on the Baltic Sea where the Germans were working on a special type of weapon, probably the forerunner of our atomic weapons.

It was a miserable, cold, wet morning at Great Ashfield when we took off. Climbing to altitude, we formed up and headed out over the North Sea. However, before we got to Helgoland, we experienced all sorts of engine troubles that Joe could not get under control. He knew that we could never reach the target and return, and he told the mission commander, who advised us to abort.

Giving Joe a heading, we begrudgingly flew back to our base. As we approached, Hardlife advised us that the field was completely socked in. We were instructed to head west, where the weather was a little better, and to land as soon as possible. In a short time, we spotted a British airfield and landed. We were greeted warmly, hustled inside and began a great three days before Headquarters could send a B-17 to pick us up.

The Brits were terrific hosts and displayed a wonderful sense of humor. Each of us was dormered in a single room, and every morning a cute WAFT would knock at the door and bring a cup of tea and a biscuit.

After breakfast, we would gather together and tell war stories. The British airmen could not understand how we could expose ourselves in broad daylight to the German fighters and ever make it back.

We were allowed to attend one of
their mission briefings, which went
like this: *"Pathfinder Mosquitoes
will depart at 1900 hours, and then
the other aircraft will depart at
intervals of two minutes, and pick*

altitude between 16,000 and 20,000   **British Pathfinder Mosquitoes**
feet. The target is the marshalling
yard southwest of Paris, and should be well marked by the time of your
arrival. Be careful, and keep your eyes open." It was hair-raising to
us. Joe Hart volunteered to go along as an observer, but no dice. As I
recall, all aircraft returned safely.

At the point we had aborted our flight, I was wearing the light-
blue heated suit that looked like a pair of long johns and fleece-lined
boots. What a ribbing I took for the several days we were there. I was
immediately dubbed the "Easter Bunny", and they never let it rest.

"Hey, Bunny, lay us an egg." *"Hey, Bunny, do you want a drink or a
carrot?"* You name it, they said it. Our hosts were a hard-drinking,
fun-loving lot. George, a quick-witted, happy-go-lucky major and an
aircraft commander whose crew duty was as a gunner, was also the
Club Officer. The bar was open just about all the time. I heard him tell
the bartender, *"If I see you taking a farthing from any of these Yanks,
you will spend the rest of the war in the kitchen."* We loved George.

The following day we attended a group meeting, where the mission
data was discussed by the ranking personnel, along with praise and
admonishments. A talk by the flight surgeon was closed with a joke
that brought loud and raucous laughter. Our bombardier, a lean
guy from Texas, told one that had them all roaring. Unfortunately,
decorum doesn't permit me from quoting it on these pages.

When we were picked up to return to base, Joe got in the left seat
and buzzed the field as a bunch of our friends waved goodbye to
their "Yank buddies".

If memory serves me, Joe and crew went down on a Berlin mission
not long after that memorable Easter Sunday. The bombardier
survived, so I believe some or all of them made it back. I thought the
world of those guys and not an Easter goes by that a little bit of "that
day" does not creep into my thoughts.

Our original crew went on and flew 28 missions by D-Day. At that time, the 30-mission cap was lifted since we were supporting the ground troops. However, Headquarters said that two crews in each squadron with the most missions could go home for a 30-day leave before returning to base. Soon, we were on orders to return home. Before our departure date, though, Al Lages, our bombardier, and I were required to report to a briefing on flying a maximum effort to "Big B" (Berlin). They didn't listen to our spouts of *"No! No! We're on orders."* We reported for duty. However, when we made it back, we swore no more runs until after our leave.

We all had our leave at home and then reported to Atlantic City to travel back to Great Ashfield. The enlisted crew members were told they were not returning to Great Ashfield. Although the officers were all sure they would also be told they were not returning to base, it wasn't long before we were on the USS America on our way to Great Ashfield. Our pilot, J. O. Leonard, obtained a job in Operations, and our co-pilot, Gene Hackel, flew C-47s, hauling personnel and cargo to the continent and back. Al Lages, the bombardier, and I flew six more missions and finished the new 35-mission limit.

Gene Hackel and his wife wrote and published "Skipper Goes to War", a tale about the trials and tribulations of smuggling our mascot, a Cocker Spaniel named Skipper, through Goose Bay before we settled in Great Ashfield.

MISSION 29, GERMAN JETS

Told by Lew Smith, Pilot, 550ᵗʰ Bomb Squadron

With Germany's frantic and headlong rush to perfect the ultimate war machine, and there wasn't any doubt that they had great equipment, the air war got down to a contest of personnel, their pride and determination. This is what ultimately enabled us to prevail. British pilots were the living, breathing examples; they fought against tremendous odds. German pilots were highly skilled veterans with two years of combat flying behind them, yet they found themselves outclassed by their British and American counterparts.

By the spring of 1945, Germany was in dire straits. Almost paralyzed industrially, its communications were badly snarled and its economy bled white. Defeat in the air, as well as on the ground, seemed to be only a matter of time. The Allied Air Force statisticians had all manner of charts, graphs and statistics to prove this was so.

Unfortunately, they could never represent with a squiggle on a graph the incredibly desperate, last-ditch flying of the German fighter pilots. A Flying Fortress shot down in flames during the last days of the war carried down to Earth, miles below, nine men who were just as dead as if they had "bought it" over Merseburg back in 1943.

Messerschmitt Me-163 – Rocket Interceptor

German Messerschmitt Me-262 – First Jet Fighter in operational service

The sight of large groups of ME-262 jet fighters and lesser numbers of the speedy ME-163 rocket interceptors still conjured up the nightmare that Hitler might yet produce a miracle in the struggle for air supremacy. The German jets were infinitely superior to any aircraft the United States had in production—or even on the drawing board. If they had been mass-produced six to nine months earlier, and if fuel and pilots had been available, they could have made a tremendous difference in the war...or, at least, in the war's duration.

On March 3, 1945, more than 50 of these new fighters playfully circled the American-escorting P-51 Mustangs at tremendous speed, then closed in and shot down six heavy bombers and three fighters without a loss. On March 18th, with the Allied victory already assured, 24 bombers and five fighters were shot down, and 16 other bombers were so badly damaged that they crash-landed in territory controlled by the Russians, who were within 50 miles of Berlin.

The 550-mph speed of the ME-262 and the punch of its four 30-mm cannons could prove devastating. One burst could tear the wing off a hapless B-17.

The March 18th mission was my 29th, and the target was Berlin, my third visit. As usual, the weather was lousy with heavy contrails at altitude. It was much like flying through soup. Fortunately, the weather did clear enough for visual bombing of the target. Just before we reached the target, ME-262 jets attacked a forward group with devastating results.

Leading the low squadron that day, I was breaking-in a new first pilot who was flying as my co-pilot. My regular co-pilot, Bill Chaney, who needed only two more missions to finish, was flying on my right wing with Lt. Cocke's crew.

Over Berlin, flak from the 400-plus anti-aircraft guns was vicious, and the smoke was so heavy that there was a gray cloud over the city. Flak put holes in nearly 700 of the 1,250 bombers on the mission.

The only good thing about a flak cloud is that the enemy fighters would seldom follow you into it. Both of my wingmen were in position as we flew into the flak barrage over the city on our bomb run.

With exploding shells bouncing the plane around, we were extremely busy trying to achieve anything resembling level flight. Under this kind of assault, the formation would spread out.

We were bombing at 27,000 feet, and even though the temperature was minus-49 degrees, one still sweats.

After dropping our bombs, we finally emerged from the cloud—battered, but still flying. However, neither wingman was with me. We had been so busy "minding our store" that we had no clue what happened to them. Later, by talking to others, we learned that my right wingman, with my co-pilot aboard, received a direct hit in their Number 2 engine, did a wing over, and started down.

We received no report on my left wingman. However, one Fortress of the four planes in our group was lost; it had exploded over the target.

The trip home to Great Ashfield was uneventful. Our battle damage was considerable, but all our fans kept turning. The Cocke crew had been from our barracks, so the return to our Quonset with their empty beds was quite a difficult experience.

It wasn't until after the war that I learned more about this mission story from my co-pilot, Bill Chaney, who had survived their crash landing. They had lost two engines over Berlin and parted company with the group. As a straggler on two engines, fighters soon hit them.

The right waist gunner was killed and the radio operator was wounded and lost his right arm, which led to his premature death a year later. At 12,000 feet, they managed to make it into a cloud cover that extended to the ground. Coming right out on the deck, an immediate crash landing was the only choice. The landing was rough and everyone was banged up, especially Chaney. He received a back injury that led to four back surgeries later.

Their crash occurred near Grodzisk, Poland, which was behind Russian lines. Picked up by the Russians, they were flown to Kiev, Russia, and locked up with about 100 other Allied air crewmen for about three months. Then, they were put on a train for a one-week ride to Odessa, where they boarded a British ship that took them to Naples. From Naples, they went to Marseilles, Paris, and finally back home to the 385th Bomb Group in Great Ashfield.

The Russians had treated them pretty much as prisoners. All in all, the round-trip took several months, but eight of the crew members finally made it home.

⭐ SILK MAPS

385th Bomb Group

Few people know about the silk maps included in the escape kits that were carried by each crewman for each mission. In 1941, many British airmen found themselves involuntary guests of the Third Reich, and the Crown was looking for ways and means to facilitate their escape. One of the most helpful aids to that end was a useful and accurate map, showing not only where things, like train stations were located, but also showing the locations of "safe houses" where an escaped POW or downed airman could go for food and shelter.

Paper maps had some real problems. They make a lot of noise when

you open and fold them, they wear out rapidly, and if they get wet, they turn to mush.

Someone in MI-5 (similar to America's OSS) came up with the idea of printing escape maps on silk. They were durable, could be scrunched-up into tiny wads and unfolded as many times as needed, and made no noise whatsoever. At that time, there was only one manufacturer in Great Britain that had perfected the technology of printing on silk—John Waddington, Ltd. When approached by the government, the firm was only too happy to do its bit for the war effort.

Map of Germany printed on Silk

By pure coincidence, Waddington was also the U.K. licensee for the popular American board game, *Monopoly*. Another coincidence was that "games and pastimes" was included in the category of items approved for insertion into "CARE" packages dispatched by the International Red Cross to prisoners of war.

Monopoly Game Box Top

Under the strictest of security, in a securely guarded and inaccessible old workshop on Waddington's grounds, a group of sworn-to-secrecy employees began mass-producing escape maps, keyed to German and Italian areas where POW camps were located.

Top Secret Document Authorizing Waddington Monopoly Games

When processed, these maps could be folded into such tiny dots that they could fit inside a *Monopoly* playing piece. As long as they were at it, the clever workmen at Waddington's managed to add a playing token containing a small magnetic compass, a two-part metal file that could easily be screwed together, and useful amounts of genuine high-denomination German, Italian and French currency hidden within the piles of *Monopoly* money!

Before taking off on their first mission, air crews were advised how to identify a "rigged" *Monopoly* set by means of a tiny red dot, cleverly disguised to look like an ordinary printing glitch and located in the corner of *Free Parking.*

Of the estimated 35,500 Allied POWs who successfully escaped, approximately one-third of them were aided in their flight by the rigged *Monopoly* games. All who did escape were sworn to secrecy indefinitely, since the British government might have wanted to use this highly successful ruse in a future war. The story wasn't declassified until 2007, when the surviving craftsmen from Waddington's, as well as the firm itself, were finally honored in a public ceremony.

It's always nice when you can play that *Get Out of Jail Free* card!

THE GOLDFISH CLUB

By Robert D. Fulkerson

Imagine surviving a ditching and then a few days later ending up a Prisoner of War in Stalag Luft III. That was how Bob Fulkerson became eligible for membership in the "Goldfish Club." The club is reserved for members of the Air Force who survive a "Ditching."

Bob first learned about the Goldfish Club while he was a POW in the North Compound at Stalag Luft III in Germany during WW II. The North Compound was predominately British POWs along with a few hundred Americans. After Bob contacted the Goldfish Club, C.A. Robertson, Honorary Secretary, mailed a membership card dated July 29, 1944, along with a black dress suit fabric Goldfish badge to his parents in Denver, Colorado, USA.

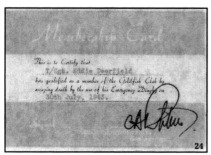 

Goldfish Club Membership Card & Arm Patch provided by Lt. Col Eddie Deerfield, Retired

This is Bob's story:

"July 29, 1944, our B-17 crew from the 351st Squadron, 100th Bomb Group, 8th AF, at Thorpes Abbott ditched our aircraft in the North Sea. Our aircraft had sustained heavy damage at the target, Merseberg, Germany, and additional damage from flak in our attempt to leave Germany. Eight of the crew survived the ditching with one severely injured gunner going down with the aircraft. We were at sea for four days before landing at Ameland, Frisian Islands, where we were taken prisoners by the Germans who met us at the beach."

A Day to Remember

July 29th 1944, the 100th Bomb Groups target for the day was the Leuna oil refinery at Merseberg in Germany. This mission was the second day in a row that the 100th bombed Merseberg. As a navigator with the 351st Squadron, 100th Bomb Group, this was my fourth mission having recently been assigned to the 100th on July 17th, 1944. Our crew was flying the B-17 'She-hasta'. Bill Greiner was flying as replacement pilot on his last mission and Jim Coccia, our regular pilot, was flying as co-pilot.

Once in Germany and arriving at the IP, we flew to the target at the altitude of 26000 feet. As we approached the target, we encountered a very dense, black carpet of flak. The flak was so thick that one would think that one could walk on it! We lost one engine as we dropped our bombs and encountered other damage forcing us to leave our formation. The entire low squadron of the 100ths A-group failed to return home along with two of the B-group of which we were one, accounting for eight B-17s lost.

Flak had knocked out the oxygen in the nose of the aircraft forcing the bombardier and me to retreat to the radio room. I had given the one walk-around bottle of oxygen to the bombardier and told him to go on to the radio room and that I would follow him. Upon entering the entrance to the bomb bay my parachute harness caught on to something and became entangled. Still being at altitude and without oxygen I soon passed out. Fortunately for me, John Vuchetich, our flight engineer, who was in the top turret, saw me and plugged in my oxygen mask. Upon recovering, I noticed that the bomb bay doors had not completely closed and upon passing out I had dropped most of my navigational aids out of the bomb bay doors. With a map or two I proceeded to the radio room. By this time we had lost a lot of altitude and while limping along, encountered more flak at about 10000 feet. Another engine was lost and Bernie Baumgarten, one of our waist gunners, was severely wounded in his abdominal area and upper left leg. Shortly after this, near Weserbunds, Germany, a squadron of P-38s (Lockheed Lightning's) appeared on the scene. Apparently they had spotted a Me 163 KOMET rocket fighter on our tail. The German pilot on seeing the squadron leaders P-38 turned in his direction until he saw the squadron leaders wingman and decided to turn away. The P-38s pursued the ME 163 and the squadron leader made direct hits and the ME 163 went down.

We continued on our way still losing altitude and soon spotted water and decided to ditch our aircraft. Hopefully it was the English Channel but it turned out we were further north and the water was the North Sea. We ditched the B-17 around noon on July 29th 1944. After surviving the ditching, John Vuchetich, our flight engineer, and I were the last two of the crew to leave the aircraft. We had remained in the radio room in hopes of saving the wounded gunner. Since the nose hatch had been opened earlier and the ball turret repositioned for ditching, water was rushing in fast and furiously. I soon realized the situation was hopeless and told John to exit the top hatch. As I climbed out the top hatch, Bernie, half covered with water, called out my name. What a feeling! From the top hatch I could see that the B-17 was at about a forty-five angle to the sea and the wings were half covered with water. As I dived into the sea and started swimming towards the two dinghies, something touched my feet. Looking back I saw it had been the tip of the B-17s rudder that had touched my feet and the aircraft disappeared from sight. Eight of us survived the ditching and Bernie sadly went down with the B-17.

We spent four days at sea. On the second day, a sailing vessel appeared on the horizon and seemingly heading in our direction, as it became closer, we fired flares and pistols into the air in hopes of attracting their attention. The ship became close enough that we could see a flag painted on the hull and took it to be Danish. What seemed like eternity, the ship proceeded on its way, choosing to ignore us and left us floundering in our frustrations. The two dinghies had been tied together to prevent our being separated. During the second night, I was awakened by the angry sea and found our dinghies starting to break apart. At the same time, John, who was in the second dinghy, awakened. He and I sat the rest of the night with our arms interlocked together. Finally daylight arrived. We had won our battle. That night has to be one of the worst nights of my life.

During the four days at sea we could hear aircraft flying over but the overcast prevented us from seeing them and in turn they seeing us. Late afternoon on the fourth day at sea, land was sighted. Separating the two dinghies, we raced, paddling to shore, firing flares into the air only to be met by German soldiers who took us prisoners. We were told, "For you the war is over!" Actually it was only the beginning. We had landed on Ameland, one of the Frisian Islands, north of Holland.

We had no food while at sea and when the Germans finally gave us some food the following day, it had been over five days since we had eaten! The Germans gave us cold potatoes and cold gravy served in two mess kits from which the eight of us took turns in eating. After a few days in Holland, of all places in solitary confinement in a convent, nine months in Germany as POWs, which included two forced marches, General Patton and his forces liberated us at Moosburg, Germany April 29th 1945.

The 100th Bomb Group was located at Station 139, Thorpe Abbotts, near Diss, some twenty miles south of Norwich, in Norfold

A few days after being liberated at Stalag VIIA, Moosberg, Germany, by General Patton and his forces, we were sent to "Lucky Strike," a transitional camp in Normandy where we were examined, de-briefed, and made ready for our departure to the U.S. We arrived in New York May 29, 1945.

ASSEMBLING THE MIGHTY EIGHTH

As told by Leslie A. Lenox, Lt. Colonel, USAF, Retired

Of all the stories that have been written and all the movies that have been shown about the 8th Air Force, very little attention has been given to what was involved in assembling the 1,200 B-17 and B-24 bombers each day, to get them in formation to carry out strikes against Germany. Certainly, showing bombers under attack by fighters or encountering heavy flak was interesting to watch, and stories about some of the rougher missions make interesting reading.

Lined up ready for take off

What was going on over England many mornings could get just as scary for the crews as the time spent over some of the targets. The coordination that had to occur during the night by the operational planners of each group, so that the crews could be briefed, was unbelievable. If the planners failed to do their jobs properly, there would have been a free-for-all among all the bomb groups in the skies over England.

The rendezvous points, altitudes, and formation times all had to be precise and known by the crews before they could get into attacking formation. The success of the planners in accomplishing their jobs enabled the 8th Air Force to become the most powerful armada ever assembled.

How this was accomplished is one of the major untold stories of the war. I was a pilot in the 95th Bomb Group in late 1944 and early 1945, and what follows is a typical mission, as I remember it, from a crew member's perspective.

Early in the evening, squadron operations would post the names of the crews scheduled to fly the following day. We could be notified two ways if our group had been alerted to fly. One was by means of lights on the front of the orderly room; the other was the raising of colored flags.

If a green light was on, the group was alerted; if a red light was on, the group was scheduled to fly; and if a white light was on, the group would stand down. The light was monitored frequently throughout the evening to learn the group's status and normally we would be notified if we were going to fly the next day.

On the morning of a mission, the CQ (Charge of Quarters) would awaken the scheduled crews about four or five o'clock, depending on take-off time. The questions we always asked were, "What is the fuel load?" and "What is the bomb load?" If his answer was "Full Tokyo Tanks", we knew that we would be going deep into Germany.

Shortly after being awakened, Army trucks would start shuttling us to the mess halls. We always had all the fresh eggs we could eat when flying a mission. After breakfast, the trucks transported us to the briefing room.

All crew members attended the main briefing, then the navigators, bombardiers and radio operators went to specialized meetings. At the main briefing, in addition to the target information, anti-aircraft locations, fighter escort, and our route in and out, we received a sheet showing our location in the group formation, the call signs for the day, and any additional information we would require to assemble our group and get into the main bomber stream.

After the briefings, we dressed into our flight gear, drew our parachutes and loaded onto the trucks for the ride to our planes. The gunners had already picked up the guns and installed them in the mounts. At this point, we were guided by the times on our daily briefing sheet. We started engines at a given time and watched for the airplanes, which would be flying in the same formation, to taxi past. We would taxi behind them, following strict radio silence.

Parked nose to tail around the perimeter on both sides of the active runway, we were extremely vulnerable to a fighter strafing attack. We were lined up on the perimeter so that the 12 planes of the high squadron would take off first, followed by the lead squadron, and, finally, by the low squadron.

At the designated time, a green flare was fired and take-off of the planes at 30-second intervals would begin. Each group had a pattern for the airplanes to fly during the climb to assembly altitude. Some would fly a triangle, some a rectangle, and some a circle. Our group flew a circle, using a "buncher" (a low frequency radio station), which was located on our field.

The patterns for each group fit together like a jigsaw puzzle. Unfortunately, strong winds aloft would sometimes destroy the integrity of the patterns, and the group's patterns would often run over each other.

Many of the take-offs were made before daylight during the winter of '44 and '45, when I was flying my tour, and it was not uncommon to climb through several thousand feet of cloud overcast. It was also quite common to experience one or two close misses while climbing through the clouds, although you would never see the other plane.

You knew you had a near miss when the plane would suddenly shake violently as it hit the prop wash of another plane. It was a wonderful feeling to break out on top, so you could watch for other planes and prevent them from running into you or into each other.

To add to the congestion we were creating, the Royal Air Force Lancasters, Halifaxes, and Wimpys would be returning from their night missions and flying through our formations. Pilots had to keep their heads on a swivel and their eyes looking out of the cockpit.

After take-off, the squadron lead would fire a flare, red-green for our group, every 30 seconds, so that we could keep him located and enable us to get into the formation. The first thing you would see when breaking out of the clouds was a sky filled with pyrotechnics, so you had to search for the group flare that would identify the lead airplane of your squadron.

Once you had it located, you could adjust your pattern to climb more quickly into formation with him. As each airplane pulled into position in the formation with the lead airplane, they would also fire a flare, making it much easier for the following aircraft to keep him in sight and join the formation.

In the mornings when the 8th Air Force was assembling, I think most crew members would agree that the pyrotechnic show in the skies over England was a rare sight to behold.

The order of progression for assembling the 8th Air Force was first to assemble the flight elements—the squadrons, groups, combat wings, divisions and, finally, into the air force.

As soon as the four squadron elements were formed, the high, low, and second elements would take up their positions on the lead element to form a squadron. When the three squadrons had completed assembly, it was necessary to form in the group position. This was accomplished by having the three squadrons arrive over a pre-selected fix at a precise time and heading. The high and low squadrons were separated from the lead squadron by 1,000 feet. After forming in a group formation, the high and low squadrons would maintain their positions by following the lead squadron.

After forming into a group formation, it was necessary to assemble into the combat wing formation. We were in the 13th Combat Wing, which consisted of three Bomb Groups: the 95th, 100th and 390th. Whichever group was leading the wing that day would arrive over a pre-selected fix at a precise time and heading. Thirty seconds later, the second group would pass over that fixed point, followed by the third group another 30 seconds later. We were then in a combat wing formation. The navigators in the lead airplanes of both the squadrons and the groups had a tremendous responsibility to ensure that the rendezvous times were strictly followed.

There were three Divisions in the 8th Air Force: the 1st, 2nd and 3rd. The 1st and 3rd Divisions consisted of only B-17s and the 2nd Division consisted of B-24s. The B-24s were faster than the B-17s, but the B-17s could fly higher; therefore, the two aircraft were not compatible for flying formation together. As a result, the 1st and 3rd Divisions flew together, and the 2nd Division flew separately.

Once the groups were flying in a combat wing formation, they would assemble into divisions. This was usually accomplished at "Coast Out"—a city on the coast selected as the departure point "Fix." The group leader in each combat wing knew his assigned position in the division, as well as the precise time that he should arrive at the "Coast Out" departure point to assume that position in the division formation.

The lead group, which had been selected to lead the 8th Air Force on this mission, would lead the first combat wing over the "Departure Fix."

Thirty seconds after the last group in the first combat wing passed that point, the second combat wing would fall in trail, and so on, until all combat wings were flying in trail and the division was formed. One minute later, the lead group in the other B-17 division would fly over that point, and the combat wings in that division would follow the same formation procedure.

When all of its combat wings were in trail, the 8th Air Force strike force was formed and on its way to the target. At the same time, the 2nd Division B-24s were assembling in a similar manner and departing to their target.

Meanwhile, as the bombers were assembling for their mission, pilots from the fighter groups were being briefed on their day's mission. Normally, 600 to 800 P-38s, P-47s and P-51s would accompany the bombers to provide protection against enemy fighter attacks. Fighter cover was not needed by the bombers until they were penetrating enemy territory; therefore, to help conserve fuel, fighter take-offs were planned to give them enough time to quickly assemble after take-off and climb on course up to the bomber groups they would be covering. The combined strength of the fighters and bombers brought the total number of aircraft participating in a mission to approximately 2,000.

A major problem that presented itself on each mission was that the bomber stream would get too stretched out. It was common for the headlines in stateside newspapers to read, *"In trying to show the strength of our Air Force."* They were referring to the fact that our first group of bombers was bombing Berlin, while the last group was still over the English Channel. It made great headlines but was a very undesirable situation.

It meant that the groups were out of position and not keeping the proper separation. Furthermore, it was almost impossible for them to get back into the desired formation. This made the bomber stream more vulnerable to fighter attacks.

Eventually, the planners determined the problem was due to the method of climbing to bombing altitude. When the first group departed the coast "Departure Fix", it would start its climb to bombing altitude. Then, as each succeeding group departed that "Fix", it, too, would begin its climb to bombing altitude.

The problem with this procedure was that as soon as the first group started its climb, its true air speed would begin to increase and it would encounter different wind velocities. Thus, it began to pull away from the group(s) following it, and the "Stretch-Out" of the bomber stream would begin.

By the time the last group reached the "Coast Out" to start its climb, the lead group would have leveled off with a true air speed approaching 250 mph and, thus, pulling away from the other groups and the bomber stream would be "Stretched-Out".

The solution to this problem that had frustrated the bomber crews was simple. The groups would no longer begin climbing at the "Coast-Out". Instead, all groups would begin climbing to bombing altitude at a designated time, irrespective of their position. Thus, all groups would have similar true air speeds and would be influenced by the same winds aloft.

Although this procedure corrected the "Stretch-Out" problem, it was still possible for a group to be out of position because of poor timing.

When one considers the technology our Air Traffic Control System has at their disposal today to guide each aircraft through the sky safely, it is unbelievable what the 8th Air Force was able to accomplish. Operating in a confined space with young air crews of minimum experience, minimum radio contact and with no ground control, the 8th launched hundreds of airplanes loaded with bombs. I would sum it up in one word: astounding.

The accomplishments of the 8th Air Force have been—and will continue to be—reviewed for many years by the historians of World War II. There will never be another air armada like it. Under the conditions of those times, the historians will never cease to be amazed at their ability to organize and launch hundreds of heavy bombers into a devastating strike force we now fondly refer to as "The Mighty Eighth."

IT'S A GRIM HARDSHIP ALL THE WAY

For the Big Bombers
From Readers Digest, 1944

The least known front on which our young men are now fighting is in the high altitude battle line. Anyone who has felt bitter cold may have some idea of the conditions on the Russian front. Movies have given a glimpse of the man who fights in a submarine or a tank. But nothing short of an actual bomber mission can tell the whole story of conditions on the 25,000-foot front. The cold is worse than Russia, the cramped quarters as bad as a tank's, the problem of oxygen as vital as in a submarine.

Leave out the danger from the enemy and consider only the natural hazards at such a great height. A bomber crew is whisked at dizzying speeds from sea level to 25,000 feet, making a deep penetration into Germany; the men are in the air from eight to ten hours, every minute packed with intensity. They must fight for their lives, possibly suffering wounds without proper medical care, and expertly control some of the most complicated and fast moving machinery ever invented.

Quick, accurate jobs had to be done by everyone from the tail-gunner to the pilot, but they have to be done in clothes that are aggravatingly bulky, for the cold may reach 60 degrees below zero. First a man dons the heaviest long underwear. Over it goes the regular clothes. Then there came the bulging, binding, winter flying-suit of leather lined with sheepskin.

He is now moving awkwardly, but there is more to come; an armor vest of steel plates, a yellow Mae West life preserver, and, over all, the parachute harness. On his head he wears a warm cap and a steel helmet. On his hands go thick heated gloves. More items remain, not clothing but gear.

Without oxygen a man would lose consciousness in about 30 seconds, so he slings an oxygen mask around his neck—later its grip on his face will be maddening. Then there are the intercom headset and the throat microphone—the one clamped over his ears, the other strapped snug around his Adam's apple.

Worry number one is take-off. The pilot is strapped into the seat by his crew chief, another restriction on movement, and he must take about 30 tons of steel and aluminum loaded with gasoline and high explosives, into the air.

From the time the throttles are advanced at the head of the runway, the tension begins. The speed mounts from 100 miles per hour to 120 miles per hour before the heavily laden plane gets off the ground. Should the plane get hit during the mission, the co-pilot is the one who won't jump. Instead he fastens his walk-around oxygen bottle, worms out of his seat, and starts aft to check the status of the crew and aircraft.

Every fold in his clothing seems to get caught on knobs, levers and corners that crowd the interior. At the deep frame of the top turret, he barely has room to squeeze by when the turret is still, but if the gunner is "searching" (rotating his turret around the horizon) he may get caught in the powered track and be seriously injured.

The narrow bomb-bay passage is fringed with sharp brackets and fixtures, and many a crew member has suffered serious cuts from them during violent action. By now his walk-around oxygen is giving out, but he continues his check of aircraft and crew.

Imagine that the right waist gunner has been wounded and is unconscious at his station. The slipstream of wind shrieks in through the open gun aperture at 60 degrees below zero. He needs a tourniquet and a compress, sulfa dust and a hypodermic. It's no job for heavy gloves. The co-pilot slips his off and if he is fast, he may be able to get the necessary procedures done in two to three minutes.

As the Forts converge toward the bomb release line, the German fighters and the anti-aircraft gunners reach their frenzied peak of resistance. The air is alive with flak. Horsing the bomber through violent evasive action takes all the strength of the pilot. The crew counts each excruciating second. Finally, the bomb run and the thrilling shout of "BOMBS AWAY".

> "The crew counts each excruciating second. Finally, the bomb run and the thrilling shout of "BOMBS AWAY."

The bomber swings from the target and turns toward home, and it goes through the same harrowing experience of fighters and flak again until that blessed moment when it slides down across the channel in the protective custody of the British Spitfires.

In spite of these fantastic hardships, no American Heavy Bomber formation has been turned back from its target by enemy action. The boys in the B-17s and B24s can take it!

Bombs Away!

★ ONE LAST MISSION

As told by Ralph D. Hollman

On Easter Sunday, April 9, 1944, I became eligible for both the Purple Heart and the Distinguished Flying Cross. The day began, as all mission days did, with an early morning wake-up call. Our crew went through the morning's activities together, as was our custom, so that we were all on the same page. First stop was the wash house to clean up and shave. Then, we walked to breakfast and the briefing of the day. The briefing indicated moderate flak over the target, which was fairly common. The next stop was the armament shack to check out our guns, which were all in order. Next, we "drew" our winter flying clothes and parachute from the central storage area, and dressed and headed out to our B-17 aircraft, "Esky".

Front Toggelier/Gunner Position

During World War II, I started my tour by flying five missions as a right waist gunner, but was then moved to toggelier/gunner when our bombardier was promoted to squadron bombardier. That Easter Sunday was to be my 25th, and final, mission. Completing 25 missions was a real achievement, especially considering that the average number of missions crews completed was 13.

The target for my 25th mission was Warnemunde on the Baltic Sea. After going on three trips to Big "B" (Berlin) in four days, I was hoping for an uneventful trip, despite the flak noted during the briefing. Take-off from Great Ashfield in England was at 0700. Our group received moderate anti-aircraft fire over the coast of France, but most of the flight to Warnemunde was uneventful. We saw no German fighter aircraft since the U.S. had gained air superiority.

Nearing the target, we started our bomb run. I was ready and waiting, as I had armed our bombs when we left the English Channel. I opened the bomb bay doors and was waiting for the signal to drop. I was recording information on time, altitude and course on a clipboard when we received an 88mm anti-aircraft shell to our Number 3 engine. Fragments from the shell pierced the nose compartment of the plane in multiple locations. Debris

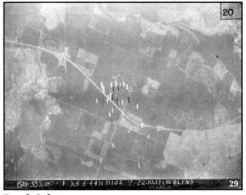

Bomb Salvo

from the shelling caused a wound to my right wrist and forearm, and my whole arm went numb. A piece of flak also penetrated my A-2 leather flying jacket and shorted out my heated suit, causing a third-degree burn to my right wrist. Despite my wounds and the crippled engine, I dropped our bombs and closed the bomb bay doors. Then, I notified the navigator that I was injured. Luckily, no one else was wounded.

As we turned toward our base, the navigator stopped my bleeding and filled my wounds with sulfur powder to prevent infection. Back at the base, I was unloaded at the end of the runway and placed in a waiting ambulance for a trip to the base hospital. After evaluating my wounds, I was transferred to the regional hospital in England. Since there were many more severely injured men in Triage, it was several hours before I was admitted to surgery.

During the initial surgery, my wounds were cleaned of debris, but were left open to heal from the inside out before final closing. I had lost the use of my right hand immediately, but after rehabilitation I was able to regain most of its function.

I remained at the regional hospital for almost two months, until June 1, 1944 when all ambulatory patients were returned to their respective units. The reason? D-Day was coming and the hospital was preparing to receive many casualties. When I returned to my unit, I continued to work on rehabilitating my hand, and I worked part-time in operations until I was returned to the States.

ONE LUCKY BASTARD

By Robert T. Marshall

I should have written something yesterday about Mission No. 1 before exhaustion shut me down for good. Now I try to catch up. In my mind, my first two missions run together and make a blur. That illustrates that I am uncertain about what really happened up there these two days, as I write this after the second mission.

The call came yesterday and it was simple: report to briefing. When he shook me awake, the sergeant said, "How did it feel?" Right now I feel like I was sleeping for 48 hours and I just don't know what really happened, like I am in a daze. So, how can I write this? I have had only one hour of sleep in the last 24 hours and I have flown two missions, but I will try to write the details.

I reacted, but it was like I was off on the side watching what was happening yesterday and not part of the action. Today's mission I can see a little clearer. When the briefing officer said Berlin was our target yesterday, he seemed to be off in another room. I was in a daze watching him, dumb and numb. The word "Berlin" had significance. It took time for me to realize we were going to drop bombs on Berlin. I can remember that much.

Chow was at midnight (2400). Briefing was at 0100. Waking in daylight to a briefing in the middle of the night put me in some turmoil. The world I was in was just plain unreal. Take-off was scheduled for 0445, in the dark. After, we had done such stuff as dressing into our flight gear, inspecting my antennas outside the plane and the equipment inside. This was Standard Operating Procedure, something I have done before, but different. We climbed to altitude, whatever that was, and assembled into the box formation that is the B-17s standard defense formation for greater firepower from the machine guns. I watched this development through the radio room window, always thinking about what might be ahead.

Departure from England, sweating and waiting kept me alert and edgy, details about which don't come to mind—I'm not sure I heard them, but I don't remember. I do remember the briefing officer said Berlin had many flak batteries protecting it. All I can say is we flew into flak, a terrible bombardment, and came out of it.

The mission lasted nine hours and 25 minutes. We were on oxygen six of those hours. When we got back, somebody counted and said we had 25 flak holes in the plane.

Billy Sunday (our tail gunner) said a piece of flak dented the three-eighths-inch armor plate he sits on in the tail and that the force of it almost knocked him off his seat. He kept talking about the ping it made. He said for a few seconds he was afraid to move his leg because he didn't think the leg was there.

We had fighter coverage—P-51s. They flew close to us and I loved seeing them out my window. After we landed, I heard someone say that the flak was the intense barrage type. At the time, I didn't know what it was like to be under a flak attack. I do now. We were bombarded from the target all the way back to the French coast. It is how the flak sounds and the fright it can create. The need to will one's self to sit there and take it as if

P-51 Escort

it's nothing unusual; that's just the way the game is played, I sense. I know the formation spread out and we dropped our bombs as we were supposed to, and I assume we did it when we were at an altitude of 25,000 to 26,000 feet.

That means we bombed the target from some five to six miles up in the sky. I know now why Ralph Armor (a friend from my hometown) acts as if he can't unwind, why he is as tense as hell. The strain really begins before take-off and it doesn't end when you crawl out of the plane after a mission. This first mission showed me that a mission is never over because there is always the next one to sweat out. Before I could absorb and sort out all that happened on No. 1, we were at it again.

Today we went to bomb Paris. Like Berlin, to me the word "Paris" had special connotations because it is a capital. I don't know if there were more or less flak guns at Paris than at Berlin. Again, I kind of blacked out on what the briefing officer said. I have to listen better at briefing. I do know that over Paris I had the thought that I had over Berlin: Get us out of this flak, Charlie! I must discipline my mind.

My wristwatch showed it was 1905 when we bombed Paris. The sunlight was of late evening. We went over the target at 21,500 feet. We hit something because smoke billowed up to almost our height. I speculate we hit an oil dump or a refinery. I have no memory of what we bombed in Berlin.

I was told that flak at the Paris target was intense. I don't know the difference yet between heavy and intense flak or how it is measured. I expect I am learning. We had about two-dozen holes in our plane from battle damage today—some of them big enough to ram a fist through. I took a long look at some of them when I walked away from the plane. I learned today that flak splattering the fuselage of a plane makes noise that sounds like rain or hailstones falling on a tin roof. Can flak be worse than what I heard today? Today a piece of flak went over Brackett's (our navigator) head, missing him by about three inches. The nose of our plane had a scar to prove it was hit.

The Paris mission was a seven-hour job. Our entry to the continent was near Cherbourg, France, some place in the area of where the D-Day invasion began. I looked hard for something I could identify as a beachhead. We were high, the clouds scattered, the sunlight weirdly weak.

I was not totally a sleepwalker today. I was quiet and I tried to act normal and observe. I studied my crew, watching their reactions. Maybe they are giving me the same treatment. Nobody is in panic. I just don't know what's going on up there. I remember bits and pieces of what happened. I also know that this is a game of survival.

The Story of Colonel Bruce Carr, 385th Bomb Group
By Bud Davisson, Flight Journal

The dead chicken was starting to smell. After carrying it for several days, 20-year-old Bruce Carr still hadn't decided how to cook it without the Germans catching him. As hungry as he was, he couldn't bring himself to eat it. Since no meat was better than raw chicken meat, he threw it away. Resigning himself to what appeared his unavoidable fate, he turned in the direction of a German airfield, believing that even POWs get to eat.

He was exhausted and tired of trying to find cover where there was none. He hadn't realized that Czechoslovakian forests had no underbrush. He had struggled out of his parachute at the edge of the farm field, never expecting to find himself a pedestrian far behind enemy lines. This never occurred to him earlier when he was screaming along at treetop level in his P-51, "Angels' Playmate". The forests and fields had been nothing more than a green blur. Messerschmitts, Focke-Wulfs, trains and trucks that he had wanted to appear in his sights didn't materialize.On this mission, he knew he was in trouble, serious trouble, when the anti-aircraft shrapnel ripped into his engine. The coolant steam hissing through the holes in his cowling told him to ride his chute down to begin a journey back to his base. A long walking tour of Czechoslovakia with Germans around him had not been part of his mission plan when he enlisted in the Army. All he had thought about was flying fighters.

Lt. Col. Bruce W. Carr, Union Springs, NY, stands by "Angels Playmate", he had claimed 22½ aerial victories by the end of WWII

By the time he enlisted, Bruce Carr
already knew how to fly, being a private
pilot since 1939. Soloing in a $25 Piper
Cub, bought by his father, he had been
instructed by an Auburn, New York,
native named Johnny Bruns. In 1942, after
he enlisted and went to meet his instructor,

AT-6 Trainer

the door opened and out stepped the man who was to be his military
flight instructor...JOHNNY BRUNS!

Bruce had this to say about
his training: *"Our advanced
training was for about four
hours and was in an AT-6.
Several of us were then told
we were going to fly P-40s
and we left for Tipton, Georgia.
The lieutenant, just back from
North Africa, showed us where*

P-40 Flying Tiger

*the levers were, made sure we knew how they worked, then said 'If you can
get it started, go flying!' Being 19 years old, knowing everything, I buzzed
every cow in that part of the state."*

Being among the first group of pilots sent to England, we were
painfully short of experience, but we learned fast enough to survive
and we were ready to move on.

Bruce's group in England was
to be the pioneering group that
would take the P-51 Mustang into
combat. Being an old P-40 pilot,
he thought flying the P-51 would
be no big deal. But he was wrong.
He was truly impressed with the
plane, stating, *"It flew like an
airplane. In a P-51, I was part of the plane and it was part of me!"*

Angel's Playmate

He went on to describe how he named his plane. *"On my first long-
range mission we kept on flying to 30,000 feet. I had gone to church as
a kid and I knew that's where the angels were, and that's when I named
my plane Angels' Playmate."*

It was then that a group of Germans roared down through Bruce's squadron. *"My leader turned for home; however, I was not that smart. I was 19 years old and I was not going to let this SOB shoot at me. We went round and round. He couldn't shake me and I couldn't get on his tail to hit him. Before long, we were within a few feet of the ground and he pulled up to go over the trees, so I pulled the trigger and kept it down. The gun barrels burned out, but one bullet, a tracer, came tumbling out, made a huge arc, came down and hit him in the left wing about where the aileron is. He pulled up, off came the canopy, and he jumped out, but too low for the chute to open and the airplane crashed. I didn't shoot him down; I scared him to death with one bullet hole in his left wing. My first victory wasn't a kill; it was more like a suicide."*

The rest of Bruce's 14 victories were much more conclusive. However, as he lay shivering in that Czech forest, any thought of being a red-hot fighter pilot was of no use to him. If he didn't get food and shelter, he was going to die.

"I knew where the German field was because I'd flown over it, so I headed in that direction to surrender. I intended to walk in the main gate, but it was late afternoon and, for some reason, I had second thoughts and decided to wait in the woods until morning.

> "On my first long-range mission we kept on flying to 30,000 feet. I had gone to church as a kid and I knew that's where the angels were, and that's when I named my plane Angels' Playmate."

While I was lying there, I saw a crew working on a Focke-Wulf-190 right at the edge of the woods. When they were done, I assumed, just like you assume in America, that the thing was all finished. The cowling's on. The engine has been run. The fuel truck has been there. It's ready to go. Maybe a dumb assumption for a young fellow, but I assumed so. So I got in the plane and spent the night hunkered down in the cockpit.

Before dawn, it got light and I started studying the cockpit. I can't read German, so I couldn't decipher dials and I couldn't find the normal switches like there were in American airplanes. I kept looking and on the right side was a smooth panel. Under this was a compartment with something I would classify as circuit breakers. They didn't look like ours, but they weren't regular switches, either.

I began to think that the Germans were probably no different from the Americans in that they would turn off all switches when finished with the airplane. I had no earthly idea what those circuit breakers or switches did, but I reversed every one of them. If they were off, that would turn them on. When I did that, the gauges showed there was electricity on the airplane.

I'd seen this metal T-handle on the right side of the cockpit that had a word on it that looked enough like 'starter' for me to think that's what it was. But when I pulled it, nothing happened, nothing. If pulling doesn't work, you push. When I did, an inertia starter started winding up. I let it go for a while and then pulled on the handle and the engine started!"

The sun had yet to make it over the far trees and the base was waking up, getting ready to go to war. The FW-190 was one of many dispersed throughout the woods, and the engine sound must have been heard by the Germans, but there was no alarm. The last thing they expected was to see their fighter taxiing out with a weary Mustang pilot at the controls; however, Carr wanted to take no chances.

"The taxiway came out of the woods and turned right towards where I knew the airfield was because I'd watched them land and take off while I was in the trees.

On the left side of the taxiway, there was a shallow ditch and a space where there had been two hangers. The slabs were there, but the hangers were gone, and the area around them had been cleaned of all debris. I didn't want to go to the airfield, so I plowed down through the ditch and when the airplane started up on the other side, I shoved the throttle forward and took off right between where the hangers had been."

At that point, Bruce Carr had no time to look around to see what effect the sight of a Focke-Wulf erupting from the trees had on the Germans. Undoubtedly, they were confused but not concerned, as it was probably a maverick pilot going against the rules. They didn't know it was OUR maverick pilot going against the rules.

He had more immediate problems than the confused Germans. He had just pulled off a perfect planejacking. However, he knew nothing about the plane, couldn't read the placards, and had to fly about 200 miles over enemy territory. Therefore, before he could head home, he had to learn how to fly the FW-190.

"There were two buttons behind the throttle and three buttons behind those two. I wasn't sure what to push, so I pushed one button and nothing happened. I pushed the other and the gear started up. As soon

as I felt it coming up and I cleared the fence at the edge of the German field, I took it down a little lower and headed for home.

All I wanted to do was clear the ground by about six inches, and there was only one throttle position for me—full forward! As I headed home, I pushed one of the other three buttons and the flaps came part-way down. I pushed the button next to it and they came up again. So, I knew how to get the flaps down...but that was all I knew.

I couldn't make heads or tails out of any of the instruments—none. I couldn't even figure out how to change the prop pitch. But I didn't sweat that, because props are full forward when you shut down anyway, and it was running fine."

This time it was the German cows being buzzed, as he streaked out over the fields and trees a few feet off the ground. At something like 350 mph, below treetop level, he tried to be a difficult target as he crossed the battle front lines. But he wasn't successful enough.

"There was no doubt when I crossed the lines because every SOB and his brother who had a .50-caliber machine gun shot at me. It was all over the place and I had no idea which way to go. I didn't do much dodging because I was just as likely to fly into bullets as around them."

When he found himself over his own airfield, he pulled up hard to set up for a landing. His mind was on flying the airplane to a safe landing.

"I pitched up, pulled the throttle back and punched the buttons I knew would put the flaps and gear down. I felt the flaps come down, but the gear wasn't doing anything. I came around and pitched up again, still punching the button. Nothing was happening and I was really frustrated."

He had been so intent on the landing problems that he forgot the tempting show he was providing the ground personnel.

"I roared around in as tight a pattern as I could fly and chopped the throttle. I slid to a halt on the runway and it was a nice belly job, if I do say so."

"As I started up the last time, I saw our air defense guys ripping the tarps off the quad .50s that ringed our airfield. I hadn't noticed the machine guns before. But I was sure noticing them right then.

"I roared around in as tight a pattern as I could fly and chopped the throttle. I slid to a halt on the runway and it was a nice belly job, if I do say so."

Bruce's antics had drawn quite a crowd, and the plane had barely stopped sliding when two MPs jumped up on the wings and tried to drag him from the airplane, not realizing he was still strapped in.

"I started throwing some good Anglo-Saxon swear words at them, and they let loose while I tried to get the seat belt undone, but my hands wouldn't work and I couldn't do it. Then they started pulling on me again because they still weren't convinced I was an American.

I was yelling and hollering. Then, suddenly they let go, and a face drops down into the cockpit in front of mine. It was my Group Commander, George R. Bickel. Bickel said, 'Carr, where in the hell have you been, and what have you been doing now?'"

Bruce Carr was home and entered the record books as the only pilot known to leave home on a mission flying a Mustang P-51 and return home flying a Focke-Wulf-190.

For several days after returning home, Bruce had trouble eating and sleeping. But when he was rested and it became a normal routine again, he took some of his fellow pilots out to show them the airplane and how it worked. One of them pointed to a small handle under the glare shield that he hadn't noticed before. When he pulled it, the landing gear unlocked and fell out. However, Bruce had figured out the important items and had landed safely back home.

Bruce Carr finished the war with 14 aerial victories on 127 missions, including three bailouts because of ground fire. He stayed in the service, flying 51 missions in Korea in F-86s, and 286 missions in Vietnam flying F-100s, for a total 509 combat missions. Make no mistake about it, Colonel Bruce Carr was definitely a fighter pilot.

Bruce Carr's stolen FW-190

DIARY OF DELIVERY

From the Diary of Lt. Charles Early

Lieutenant Charles Early was a pilot of a B-17 in the 91st Bomb Group. He was shot down on a mission to Solingen in the Ruhr Valley on December 1, 1943, and was sent to Stalag Luft One. He kept a very complete journal during his confinement. Gary Early, his son, gave permission to print Lt. Early's "Diary of Delivery", his vivid word picture of the final couple of weeks at Stalag One.

"APRIL 20, 1945: Adolph Hitler's birthday. I am told by the Germans that there have been great celebrations among the populace. Most flattering, a salute rendered by the Russians who laid down an artillery barrage from 0200 to 0800, somewhere within hearing distance of here, Stettin, most likely.

LATER IN THE WEEK: Russians have reached Berlin, and are advancing into the city in their best steamroller fashion. Hitler has been reported to be in the front lines of the city's defenses, so the fall of Berlin will probably bring an end to this war.

APRIL 25: Heavy artillery fire from the south at 2045, continuing at intervals through the night. FW-190s and ME-109s at the airfield at Barth—tactical aircraft, so front must not be far away. We estimate 40-50 miles, from the sound of the firing.

APRIL 29: Short air raid at 1240. Guns sound louder. Saw our first Feiseler "Storch", a reconnaissance aircraft for artillery spotting.

APRIL 30: This morning we started walking guard in the compound. I will have a squad as soon as we take over. Col. Zemke came over and started the boys digging foxholes. Himmler is reported to have his headquarters just across the bay, Goering with him. Hitler has died in Berlin. All the planes are leaving the airfield, and demolition has commenced. German Intelligence department has left. Barth is being evacuated. Russians reported 20 to 25 miles away, driving like mad; we can see smoke from the airfield.

APRIL 30 at 1600: The Germans are blowing up installations at the Flak School by the South Compound, also the factory west of there. The demolitions get louder and occur at more frequent intervals. It gives one a queer feeling to see Germany fall to pieces before one's eyes. Rumors are flying around so fast that I can't keep up with them. Several Russian pilots were shot down at Stralsund and were brought to this camp. They say that Joe will be here tonight. I shall not undress. All lights went out about 2300.

MAY 1: 17 months a prisoner today. Very fitting that I should be awakened this morning at 0500 by the fellows raising a hell of a racket. Looked out the window, and there are American guards in the towers. It leaves me a little numb. I just can't believe it.

Seems that the Germans stole silently away last night under cover of darkness, so, after all the talking and planning, we have finally taken over the camp.

Now we wonder when the Russians will arrive. Major Blum and Col. Sluga came over about 0500 and shot the bull a bit. Everybody was excited! Wonder where the Kommandant and his staff went, and if Himmler is still on the peninsula. Know that in the future that when I read this, I shall be appalled at its coherency, but things happened so damned fast that my head is spinning...more than somewhat.

Now that it is practically over and I look back at the whole period, I find that it has not been so terrible. Of course, the months of famine when we had no food or cigarettes were pretty grim, usually we had enough food and with a wonderful cook like Trubia, we really ate quite well. Our bridge sessions with Col. Sluga and Major Blum have been a lot of fun, as have our crazy discussions.

I believe that I am a mature, levelheaded person and more fitted to tackle life in the future. Underneath all the joy, however, lies a feeling of sadness at the thought that I may never see the fellows I've lived with and scrapped with for over 3 years. What a hell of a good bunch here in my room.

MAY 1st at 0830: I listened to the British Broadcasting Corporation on the barracks speakers. How wonderful to hear English spoken instead of the old harsh German! Col. Zemke made a short talk. We're taking over the camp today. This afternoon we're passing through another low feeling... an anti-climax. All sorts of rumors have been going around. Russians are 3 kilometers away. Burgermeister commits suicide.

MAY 1ˢᵗ at 1020: A damned historic moment. The Russians have really arrived!! The camp has gone mad. The main body's reported to be four or five hours away. German radio announced the death of Hitler… at long last. Listened to BBC again. They played the Star Spangled Banner. My God, what a moment! All the men came out of their rooms and stood attention in the hall, tears running down their faces, some of them sobbing. More important goings-on should take place tomorrow. I'm dead!!

Did I say the Russians have arrived? My God, they took over the place! In order to keep us from roaming over the peninsula, the American Senior Officers have locked up the place tighter than it ever was. A mistake, I'm afraid. The fences were torn down today on orders from a Russian who said he was a colonel.

He raised a hell-of-a-row about us being locked up, and brandished a pistol more than somewhat. (He was later exposed as a corporal.) We all went barreling across to Barth to see what the place looked like at close range. The Russians greeted us wildly, and wine actually flowed in the streets.

They have tanks drawn up in the square, have taken all automobiles, horses, etc. and there is great activity. The populace looks quite different than it did when we arrived here a year and a half ago. There are reports of looting and rape by the Russians, but rape seems a little on the order of wasted effort, as the Frauleins are most generous.

The village people seem to be glad that we're here, after seeing the Russians. Visited the concentration camp, which will forever remain in my memory as the most horrible sight I have ever seen!! The place was surrounded by electrically charged wire, and inside were freshly dug graves, which the inmates had prepared for some of the more fragrant inmates. The filth in the living quarters was indescribable.

The floor and walls were covered with human offal, and over the whole place hung a sickish sweet odor… an odor which I have never before smelled, but which is instinctively recognized as death. And, indeed, the place was filled with death. We went into rooms where all the inmates were dead. Sitting up in chairs, sprawled on their bunks, or crumpled on the floor, starved to death.

Not 1,000 feet away was the post hospital, a beautiful establishment with very modern medical aid, but it was denied to these poor wretches. I talked to some of the Frenchmen who had been here for years (I found it was very difficult to speak French without lapsing into German every now and then).

We brought the helpless ones out and carried them to the hospital where they were bathed and put into clean beds, and treatment begun. Many of them were too far gone, however, to save. The most shocking thing was the number of women there.

MAY 10: The Russians have rounded up the cattle of the area and have driven 150 Holstein cows into our camp. We're eating steaks!! Ah, luxury!! We still don't know when the Americans are coming for us. It's been 12 days since we were freed, and still they haven't come.

MAY 12: They've come!!! Started arriving at 2:00 PM today. My old group, the 91st Bomb Group, was the first to arrive. Have found that I will leave tomorrow.

MAY 14, RHEIMS, FRANCE: At last, it has happened. I am out of Germany. We were marched from camp this morning, through Barth to the airdrome, and were flown here. We came over the Ruhr. I don't believe it! Huge cities like Essen, Dusseldorf, etc., can't be so completely annihilated. It's numbing!

We will go from here tomorrow to a camp, of all things, 'Camp Lucky Strike', which is at St. Valery en Caux between Le Havre and Dieppe. We expect to ship from Le Havre and go straight to New York... and then home!!! That is all! Over and out!!!"

By Charles Hamlin

I thought, if I didn't buy the farm on the Zwickau raid, I was missing a hell of a good chance to buy it. This was probably the most fighters and the most flak, except Berlin, that I ever saw. The Germans threw everything they had at us. There must have been something the Germans didn't want bombed. They did everything possible to prevent the bombing, but to no avail. The bombs were dropped and dropped accurately.

The first wave of German fighters, FW-190s and ME-109s, assembled in front of the formation at about a thousand yards or so. They were flying around in tight circles, getting ready for a head-on run at us. There must have been 30 or 40 of them in the first wave. They were trying to turn us away from our target. The group endured several attacks, which kept getting heavier and heavier. The fighters attacked for what seemed like the whole mission, but quit when we started our bomb run. We only had to contend with heavy flak for the next 20 minutes or so.

(top): German Focke-Wulf-190
(bottom): German ME-109s in flight

This was the best defense we ever put up while I was flying. I think the fact that we could see the fighters milling around in front of us prior to forming and coming in is what gave us time to form a "solid wall" formation, rather than our "spread out" formation. It gave most of our gunners the opportunity to fire at the fighters without worrying so much about hitting one of our own. Never was I so glad to be back from a mission as I was from Zwickau. Only Berlin was comparable.

The best part of this mission, and all other days of a mission (assuming you got home in one piece), was a debriefing crew anxiously waiting. They were cheerful, polite and treated you like a returning hero. The debriefing started with a good stiff shot of scotch whiskey, even two shots if you could get in line just behind a non-drinker. This was a feat one managed to accomplish after every mission, if one was a scotch lover.

Next was the debriefing itself, where we were encouraged to talk freely about the mission (after two shots of scotch, one didn't need much encouraging). We claimed every enemy fighter that came anywhere near our formation. We reported on the enemy aircraft shot down or damaged the number of aircraft seen, flak intensity, our own losses, details of any crewmen appearing to have bailed out, and the amount of damage done to the target. We were asked to estimate the percentage of bombs landing on the target, or within 1000 yards of it, and, finally, any problems with our aircraft. The next stop was the mess hall (this would be our first food since about 6 am that morning). Again, you would try to get behind a light eater.

On the Zwickau raid we lost a large number of airplanes. Many parachutes were counted headed down where only a future as a prisoner of war was waiting for them. Many remained prisoners for a few years. The camps, or "Stalags", were numerous and mostly in Germany, but also found in other countries. In none of them were you treated like anything other than as one of the enemy.

Amazingly, they were made up, almost exclusively, of flying crews, both American and British. Since the major ground attacks against German troops did not start until after D-Day in 1944, there were no Allied ground troops captured except in North Africa and southern Italy.

Fortunately, many of our crewmen kept a detailed diary of their experiences while imprisoned. These diaries are so important for our future generations so they will not forget the sacrifices made by the men and women who served.

MISSION TO BRUX

By Hugh S. Andrew

The missions to Germany were long and dangerous, and many of the targets in German-occupied Europe were very well protected by both anti-aircraft batteries and fighters. One of the most difficult was Bordeaux, France, where the Germans had a large submarine operation. It was very important that we try to destroy submarine pens in order to take the pressure off our trans-Atlantic supply lines. The very existence of England depended on these supplies arriving in a timely manner. Recently, I was reminded about one of the missions I had been a part of and it brought back memories.

An article came across my desk a few days ago about a little town in Czechoslovakia named Brux. We went to that town one day in the summer of 1944 to bomb a synthetic oil plant. It started out like any other mission. Someone woke you at 4 a.m. for the mission, and he told you the gas load and the bomb load, but not the target. If there were full gas and bomb loads for the planes, you knew you were going a long way, but you didn't know where. You got up and went to the mess hall for breakfast and then to the briefing room. There was a map on the wall, hidden by a curtain. After everyone got seated and quieted down, the briefing officer pulled the curtain aside and you saw the map of Europe with tape outlining the route, in and out, and the target location. We were going to fly all the way across Germany to the target: Brux, Czechoslovakia (there was a loud groan from all when this was seen).

After the crew briefings (pilots, navigators, bombardiers and radio operators) were completed, we all proceeded out to our planes and did our pre-flight checks. Our pilot for this mission was from the 551st Bomb Squadron, and he was flying his last mission. He had replaced our own pilot, Wes Brashear, who had been with our crew since it was formed but was scheduled to go into lead crew training.

We took off as scheduled, assembled in formation, and started climbing. At 15,000 feet, we crossed the English Channel and approached the coast of continental Europe. Suddenly, our Number 4 engine started to miss. We attempted to enrich the fuel mixture and to switch to other gas tanks, but nothing seemed to help. The engine would get progressively rougher the higher we climbed However, since we couldn't do much about it, we took what we could get out of it and kept on going.

We finally reached bombing altitude and were basically flying on three engines, which at least kept us in formation. We certainly didn't want to drop out of formation deep inside Germany. During the bomb run we encountered some flak, but dropped our bombs on the target. After the bombs were released and as we were turning away from the target—BOOM! The propeller on the Number 3 engine ran away and the RPM was out of control. We tried to feather it, but failed. We were concerned that it would go completely out of control, freeze up and pull the engine from the wing.

We couldn't stay in formation since we couldn't maintain a speed of 150 mph. We left the formation and maintained radio silence since any transmission we would make to the group leader could be picked up by an enemy ground radio station. This would have advised the Luftwaffe that there was a crippled aircraft that could not stay with its group.

We turned back to the west and gradually lost altitude. We discovered that by flying at 110 mph we could keep the propeller from windmilling. Over 110 mph, the prop would start to run away. In the meantime, Number 4 was barely running. Here we were—two good engines, one running only a third of the time, and one totally stopped. We were gradually losing altitude. Our only hope was that we could reach a part of Belgium that was under the control of the Allies.

This was one particularly beautiful day over Europe. There wasn't a cloud in the sky anywhere, high or low. Soon, all the planes in our group, and all the other groups, were gone. We could see a hundred miles in all directions, and every German within a hundred miles could see us.

There was no place to hide; we were "sitting ducks". However, as we descended in altitude, there was a reverse effect on the Number 4 engine and it began to run better. We began to think that we could stretch our flight, and possibly get to the English Channel, where we might ditch.

Then, without warning, a lone P-51 appeared beside us and for the next half-hour it escorted us toward England. For a P-51 to fly at 110 mph, he had to put his flaps down and reduce his power to barely above stalling speed. After a half-hour, he waved to us, indicating he was low on fuel and must leave us and head back to England.

P-51 Bomber Escort

At an altitude of 3,000-4,000 feet, we now felt that we could hold our altitude, so we kept going. It seemed we might make it back to England. We maintained radio silence and kept going. Finally, we crossed the channel and arrived back at Great Ashfield and the 385th Bomb Group. We made our landing and parked. I can tell you that our pilot, who flew his 35th and last mission, was one happy fellow.

We never did find out what happened to our Number 4 engine, but we did find out what caused the Number 3 engine to run away. A small piece of flak had cut a quarter-inch diameter line that supplied hydraulic fluid to the propeller feathering system, making it impossible to feather the prop.

MY FIRST MISSION

By Howard T. Richardson

After enlisting in the Army Cadet program in 1942, I graduated as a pilot and received my commission as a second lieutenant in August 1943. I requested multi-engine training and was assigned to B-17 transition. Completing B-17 training, I was assigned to Salt Lake City to pick up my crew of six airmen and three officers. After completing our crew training, we were directed to Grand Island, Nebraska, to pick up a new B-17G, which we flew—with several stops along the way—to Nulls Corner, Ireland. During our flight, we witnessed the beautiful Northern Lights.

Leaving our new aircraft in Ireland, we proceeded by water and rail to the 385th Bomb Group at Great Ashfield, England. We flew a few practice missions to acquaint us with the local area and to practice flying close air formation. Group policy was to have new crews co-pilot with an experienced combat crew.

Scheduled to fly on our first combat mission, we were awakened after midnight. After dressing, we proceeded to the mess hall for a breakfast of powdered eggs (two fresh eggs, if flying a mission), powdered milk, Spam, SOS, British bread and marmalade, and plenty of coffee or tea.

After breakfast, we headed to the briefing building for a general briefing. The wall was covered with a curtain and when the Group Commander, Colonel Elliott Vandevanter, arrived, the curtain was opened to reveal the route to and from the target. The target was Zwickau, Germany, and all present gave a loud groan. Zwickau was deep in Germany and south of Leipzig and Dresden. Total flight time was eight hours and 45 minutes.

We were briefed on weather conditions and known anti-aircraft positions and fighter locations. All present set our watches to Greenwich Time; navigators, bombardiers, radio operators and lead crews went to special briefings. The gunners picked up the guns and ammunition and we proceeded to the assigned aircraft. The aircraft was fueled and the bombs had been loaded by the armament bomb crew. The bomb load for this mission was five 1,000-pound demolition bombs.

When the tower shot a flare, we all taxied to the active runway, following the lead aircraft. At the proper time, the tower shot another flare and the lead aircraft started his take-off. Other aircraft followed in 30-second intervals and joined in their assigned spot in the formation, and the group continued on course en route to the target after joining other bomb groups positioned five minutes apart.

The following times and the number of enemy fighters were taken from the official mission report that was submitted by our intelligence officer to higher Headquarters:

At 1207 hrs, our first wave of enemy fighters appeared, 20 FW-190s and ME-109s making a head-on attack, a 10 o'clock and a 2 o'clock, coming back three times. The second wave came at 1230 hrs with 40 to 50 ME-109s and FW-190s. This wave continued to hit the groups behind us.

The third wave hit at 1425 hrs and contained 60 to 70 ME-109s and FW-190s. The last, or 4th wave, of 20 to 25 FW-190s attacked from 11 o'clock to 1 o'clock, and started concentrating on stragglers or bombers that could not keep up with the formation because of damage to their aircraft.

When we turned on the "IP" (Initial Point), the beginning of the bomb run, we began receiving anti-aircraft flak, which continued until we dropped our bombs and turned off the target course.

On this mission, our group claimed 11 German fighters, destroyed six probable and one damaged. Our crews also reported seeing a B-17 going down, 10 chutes sighted, and one B-17 that caught on fire and fell on another B-17. A German fighter shot down by our group fell into a B-17, and they both exploded. Only the tail gunner appeared to escape with his chute.

The bombing results for the group were excellent, with all bombs falling within a 1,000-foot circle. The group later received a Presidential Unit Citation for these bombing results. Crew comments made after this mission were that the close formation flown by our aircraft on this mission saved the group's planes from greater battle damage from the German fighter aircraft.

The return flight was made watching for fighters and flak, and taking evasive action when necessary. When we approached the English Channel and saw the white cliffs of Dover, we started our decent and flew over our field, peeling off one at a time. Aircraft that had wounded on board or severe damage were given priority and landed first.

After landing, parking the aircraft and debriefing the intelligence by providing the details of the mission (i.e., fighters, flak sighted, fighter attacks, etc.), we proceeded to the mess hall and then to our barracks for much-needed rest for another mission the next day.

Not seeing our crew co-pilot, who had flown with another crew, I discovered that he was in the B-17 that shot the German fighter that then collided with it and exploded.

After this mission, we received a new B-17G. Since I was the pilot and from Mississippi, the crew named the plane "Mississippi Miss". It survived the war and was eventually retired at the U.S. storage facility at Davis Monthan AFB in Tucson, Arizona. Our crew went on to complete 35 combat missions and we all received a certificate titled, "The Lucky Bastard Club".

Some of our following missions were to Hamburg, Hamm, Hanover, Wesermünde, and three missions to Berlin. We started flying combat missions on May 12, 1944 and flew our 35th mission on August 11, 1944. After completing my 35th mission, I was assigned to the 4th Bomb Wing as an operations officer for a period of seven months. In April 1945, I returned to the United States.

By Stewart H. Day

We left our base at Great Ashfield, England, in the early morning for Bordeaux, France, to bomb the submarine pens. However, the target was clouded over, so none of our incendiary bombs were dropped.

Over Biscay Bay, on our way back to England, we had engine trouble and dropped back about three or four miles from our formation. Dropping the bombs in the sea, we were attacked by two German fighters who came out of the sun. Both fired at the same time, one low and one high, over and under my position in the tail. The waist, ball turret, radio room, as well as the engines and vertical tail were hit hard, and all of the men in those areas were wounded.

The first call on the intercom was to bail out, but Walter Olowniuk, the radio operator, remarked that we were going to ditch. The pilot, Theodore Kleuser, turned the plane and headed toward the shore. In the radio room, the extra rafts, parachutes, ammo boxes, and the floor itself were on fire. As Olowniuk threw them into the waist, I threw them out the door.

The ball turret gunner, Stanley Wysokinaki, and the two waist gunners, James O'Keefe and Leo DeGraw, were down on the floor, badly wounded. Having put out the fire and dropping from 25,000 feet without oxygen, Olowniuk and I were too exhausted to help the wounded men. We ditched without any further injuries.

The bombardier, Tom Betow, and navigator, Frederick Albert, came into the plane's waist area and helped the three wounded men into rafts. One of the German aircraft flew over us, but did not fire. Each raft held five men. Raft #1 held Walter Olowniuk, Stanley Wysokinaki, Frederick Albert, Theodore Kleuser and me, Stewart Day. Raft #2 held John Slater, Thomas Betow, Earnest Hibbard, Leo DeGraw and James O'Keefe.

Suddenly, my raft began to receive sniper fire from the shore. We all jumped overboard. The pilot, Kleuser, stood up and was shot in the head. Fred Albert was also shot. In waves that were two to three feet high, I lost my grip on Stanley and Fred and never saw them alive again. After a number of hours, a German air rescue plane landed and picked us up from the raft. John Slater was dead from either a gunshot or drowning. Albert died in the first-aid room. Raft #2 drifted toward shore and I lost track of what happened to them. I heard rifle shots and machine gun fire from the shore,

As I was interrogated, the Germans wanted to know how many men were on the aircraft. I told them 10 men. They sent out a seaplane to look for more men and picked up Tom Betow. I had a bad feeling that they would kill everybody that made it to shore.

Our trip to a POW camp is another story. Walter and I were sent to camp 17B, located in Krems, Austria. Tom Betow was sent to an officer's camp, Luft 3. I later learned that the soldiers who shot at us while in the rafts were from India. They had been captured in North Africa and were now fighting for the Germans.

There were three survivors: Tom Betow, Walter Olownick, and myself. For this mission we had been assigned to a B-17 that our crew had never flown before and, since it was before daylight when we boarded and the flight ended by ditching, we never knew the plane's name.

THE LAST MISSION OF RUM DUM

By Roy Jillson

On April 10, 1945, we flew our 15th mission with Lt. Muchow as our pilot and Lt. Kokus, flying his 35th and final mission to close out his tour of duty, as our co-pilot. Once again, we were flying "Rum Dum", one of the most famous B-17s in the 8th Air Force for completing 105 missions without an abort. Her ground crew and the base commander were out to capture the all-time record of non-aborted missions by one aircraft. Little did we know that this was to be Rum Dum's last mission.

"Rum Dum"

Our target for the day was a jet fighter base in the vicinity of Berlin. I was at the right waist gun position and Buck Krouse was manning the left waist gun as we began the bomb run. We were both on the lookout for German fighters, as it was a beautiful, sunny day...just right for a fighter attack.

We crossed over the air base at 15,000 feet, rather than the usual 25,000 feet, per General Doolittle's instructions to observe the severe damage that had already been inflicted by the bombers ahead of us. Our bombs exploded on a hanger and on a row of brick barracks.

About 15 minutes after "bombs away", Buck and I released the cord of our flak suits, as we had not been briefed on some possible uncharted flak. No sooner had our suits hit the floor when the guys up front of the plane called out, "Flak at 12 o'clock level!" We were flying right into the shells that were exploding. Buck and I saw the bursts from the windows in the waist. Big, black, coughing, puffing bursts! Not many, but right up there with us. It was a bit late to get back into our flak suits.

We heard three distinct slams against the plane within the next minute and we heard pieces of flak tearing through the ship. I smelled smoke right away and looked forward toward the radio room to see if that was the location of the fire. Unplugging my heated suit and hooking on to a portable oxygen tank, I went forward to check.

While off intercom, Mick Cooper, our engineer, had let us know that there was a fire under his gun turret. A shell fragment had made a hole about two inches in diameter outside and peeled back the armor plating inside, producing a hole about the size of a man's head. Wood splinters and metal had sprayed all through the nose section, and set fire to two A-3 bags filled with clothing.

Another direct hit caught the Number 1 engine. Lt. Muchow tried to feather the prop, but to no avail. The engine started smoking and throwing oil while the prop windmilled and ran away. By this time, we realized we were pretty badly damaged as the shells continued to explode around us. We had dropped out of formation and called for fighter support. Checking the battered plane for further damage, we found holes about two feet from the fuselage in each of the tail's horizontal stabilizers. There were many other hits around the tail, and the tail gunner notified the pilot that there was excessive vibration all through the tail section.

Buck and I noted a large flak hole close to where we had been standing, and we saw a number of holes on the left and right wings. Our navigator, Jack Shearman, who was standing at the time, noted a 1.5-inch hole just to left of the chin turret that entered the nose and careened out the top. He believes the fragment would have hit him between his arm and body if he had been seated at his desk.

After checking with all crew members for injuries (none reported), we came down to 10,000 feet and removed our oxygen masks. We were still over enemy territory, so the navigator plotted a course to the nearest friendly airstrip. Lt. Muchow gave us the choice of bailing out or staying with the ship; however, he wished to continue flying until we reached an area taken over by Allied forces.

He reminded us that German farmers in the region were known to shoot airmen on their way down in their chutes or to run a pitchfork through those who landed. Although Rum Dum was a tired old veteran even before we took off, now she was a rambling wreck. Still, we had faith in the old B-17 and for that reason, to a man, we decided to ride her down, rather than bail out.

By that time, we had three P-51s barreling around us, looking for any German fighter hungry to take on a straggler like us. I left the waist gun and returned to the radio room. Lt. Shearman gave me the code name of a friendly landing strip where we proposed to land. I prepared and sent a message, in code, to our division station outside London, identifying our plane, advising them of our intended landing site, and that all crewmembers were without injury. The message was acknowledged, so all appeared well.

"Rum Dum" Nose Damage

However, while I was off intercom and on radio, the Number 1 engine started to flame and Buck advised me to get on the intercom. Our left wing was vibrating badly and Lt. Muchow told us to standby to bail out.

He advised the members in the nose that the Number 1 engine prop was apt to fly off, and they were to go to the radio room and prepare for an emergency landing. Mick Cooper, a bit shaken from the blast of flak beneath his top gun turret, came through the bomb bay into the radio room with his souvenir. In his hand was a jagged fragment of a shell about the size of a quarter-pound of butter.

With the two pilots at the controls and the remaining seven crewmen jammed up against each other in the radio room, we awaited the emergency landing. Lt. Muchow greased us in on the steel mat runway, and a British fire truck arrived and put out the fire in Number 1 in a matter of minutes.

We had landed at Typhoon fighter-bomber strip, commanded by the British. The pilots, British, Canadian and South African, were using this airstrip for short-range bombing and strafing sorties. It had been taken over by the Allied forces only three weeks prior to our touchdown. Since Rum Dum was no longer on fire, Lt. Muchow fired up two engines and I transmitted a corrected message to London, advising them of our landing and our condition. No one wanted to be listed as Missing in Action.

After stripping Rum Dum of everything secret and movable, we accepted the hospitality of our British hosts.

A South African pilot, who had just returned from a sortie, showed me the cockpit of his fighter. We were asked about our bombing mission of the day, and noticed the crowd of men gathering around Rum Dum, admiring the many bombs painted on her nose—one for each of her over 100 missions—and the many swastikas that recorded verified German fighters downed by her many crew members during her prior trips.

As we left the airstrip by an English lorry, we noticed the road was lined with foxholes and pillboxes. We passed American and German graves, burnt-out tanks and overturned cars. We passed through small villages completely blasted to rubble, with houses, churches and a beautiful windmill all in ruin.

We passed through Holland and then back into Germany. Toward midnight near some tents on an airbase, we were given some C-rations for supper, then some cots with good old wool blankets.

The next day, after an early lunch of pork chops and apple pie, we boarded an open Army truck for a five-hour trip to Brussels, Belgium, where we could hitchhike an air ride back to our base in England.

We were dropped off at a private school, a haven for persons in our situation. After dinner and a shower, we received passes to visit Brussels until midnight. Our only clothing was our high-altitude flight gear.

The Belgian people welcomed us with hugs and kisses wherever we went. A Belgian gentleman who spoke English recommended we visit a famous fountain in the city of Brussels, which we did. It was a large stone fountain filled with water and the figure of a naked boy who was peeing into the water.

I believe the statue was called "Manneken Pis." According to the story, the statue is of a child of royalty peeing in the direction of the enemy and, thus, turning the tide of the battle. After further exploring Brussels, we flagged down an Army truck and returned the seven miles back to the school.

After a sound night's sleep, we had a rousing breakfast and then left Belgium in a British C-47 ambulance plane. A B-24 crew that had crash-landed the previous day and a wounded P-51 pilot were also on board. Instead of a group of casualties on the plane, we were a group of rowdies to the English nurses aboard. On our arrival back in England, the parting words of a pretty English nurse were, "Ohhhh, you Yanks!"

It was good to get back to the base and letters from home. No doubt, Lt. Kokus was the happiest of us all. He had finished his tour and was looking forward to being back home in Indiana.

My Next to Last Mission

By Joel D. Punches

February 21, 1944 - We were bombing Hamburg, Germany, at 25,000 feet on my next-to-last mission (No. 24). Over the target, we were hit by flak from the ground that knocked out two engines. We had to leave the formation and drop down and back. Ten minutes later, two German fighter planes spotted us and attacked us head on. They knocked one more engine out. We then were at 6,000 feet and going down at 1,000 feet a minute with one engine on fire.

The German fighter planes were circling and getting ready for the kill, so we decided that if we kept flying, we would never get back to England and might have to ditch in the channel. In the winter, that was close to suicide.

We bailed out through the bomb bay. I was sure that we were over Holland rather than Germany. I hit the ground and hid my parachute, opened my escape kit, got out my compass and silk map, and started walking southwest.

I walked to the nearest farmhouse, and the lady there showed me where I was on the map. I walked for four hours and met a Dutchman on a bicycle, who I stopped. When he finally realized who I was, he put me in a ditch to hide and came back for me at 10 pm. He then took me to a house, where I stayed for one week. While I was there, they gave me civilian clothes and a false ID card that indicated I was a druggist from Amsterdam.

I was told to go to Spain, where I would be free. Following another Dutchman, I traveled by train. At night, I stayed with safe Dutch people. I had to walk across the Holland-Belgium border, and I stayed in a haystack for one week.

I got as far as Liege, Belgium, when the Allied invasion started. I was told to stay put and wait for the U.S. 1st Army to arrive. Then, I was free. I had many interesting experiences while traveling around. At one train station I ate dinner with two German soldiers and I never said a word.

Crossing river bridges was always an experience. There were German guard houses on both sides and every 10 to 15 people were pulled in and interrogated. I finally figured it out and I timed it so I was always the first or second to go by the guardhouse.

I stayed in many towns in Holland—Rosemont, Venia, Eindhoven, and Ermelo. In Roermond, I stayed one month in a house without looking out a window the whole time.

From Liege, I rode in an Army truck to Paris, where I was flown back to London. In London, I was promoted one rank, given $1,500 in back pay, a new uniform, and put on a boat to New York.

Later, I found out Lapstresky, our co-pilot, was shot down February 22, 1944 over the North Sea. He is buried in Holland.

NAVIGATING THE NORTH ATLANTIC

By Paul Tanksley

It's a pity we don't think of all the losses and hardships that a war causes BEFORE the war. In order to attack Germany with several thousand aircraft, we had to get those aircraft to England. This was a perilous job for young, inexperienced crewmen who had no idea how to fly across an ocean.

Many bombers were lost on these trips. There were two main routes: the northern route and the southern route, and each had their dangers. The northern route went from Bangor, Maine, to Newfoundland, Iceland, Scotland, and sometimes Greenland, depending on winds aloft. The southern route was from West Palm Beach, Florida, to Trinidad; Belem, Brazil; and Casablanca, Morocco, again depending on winds.

Late in 1944, Capt. Daniel L. Boone and navigator Willie Leveen were at Santa Maria, Azores, preparing their Douglas C-54 transport for a flight to Ayr (Prestwick), Scotland. Boone had flown the mail since the open-cockpit days of the early 1930s. Leveen had been a flight radio officer on the North Atlantic routes for several years, but had recently switched to the position of navigator and was making his fifth crossing.

The standard flight plan route called for a great circle track from Santa Maria to 50'N, 7'30"W. The flight would then alter course slightly to fly over St. George's Channel and across the Irish Sea toward Prestwick. The trip would be about 1,500 nautical miles and would require about nine hours of flying time. They knew a cold front was approaching Great Britain from the west, but the weather forecast did not call for the front's arrival at Prestwick until about one hour after the flight's ETA of 0100 GMT.

The flight departed Santa Maria about 1600 GMT with a flight crew of five, a purser and 18 passengers. Shortly before 2200 GMT, Willie Leveen noticed a mass of clouds ahead—the forecasted cold front was obviously moving faster than anticipated. He quickly shot a four-star fix while the C-54 was still in the clear. The fix showed the plane to be on course with a revised ETA of 0105.

Once the plane entered the clouds, radio bearings and dead reckoning were the only navigational options. About 2300 GMT, Hoag, the radio operator, got a fix from a ground radio station at The Valley, Wales. When Leveen plotted the LOP, it was just about at a right angle to the projected course. Willie scratched his head. If the fix was correct, the airplane's ground speed had been drastically reduced.

About 2400 GMT, Leveen approached Captain Boone and asked if he would climb out of the clouds so he could take a star shot. *"Not a chance,"* Boone reportedly responded. He was concerned that the clouds rose to extreme heights and he didn't want to waste fuel.

Leveen returned to his chart table. According to the flight plan, it was time to catch the eastern leg of the Nutt's Corner (Belfast) LF radio range aid and ride it in to Prestwick, but the radio signal could not be found. Leveen pondered his predicament: no definite fix and fuel burning at a rate of 240 gallons per hour. Leveen went again to Boone and renewed his request. Boone again demurred, not only for the original reason but also a celestial fix would be of little help in landing at Prestwick. Leveen and Hoag continued to monitor all radio frequencies. Occasionally signals could be heard, but none could provide an LOP.

The flight crew was aware of their predicament. Those in the passenger cabin, however, were unaware of the mounting problems. The safety of the aircraft rested in the hands of Daniel L. Boone. He consulted with Leveen and both reasoned that the Irish Sea must lie to the west of their current position. Boone suggested that the aircraft turn to a westerly heading and descend to the point where it would break out of the clouds over water.

Perhaps from that point the plane could find its way to Prestwick visually. Boone pulled back the four throttles, turned to a heading of 270, and watched as the altimeter unwound.

The altimeter's pressure setting had not been adjusted since reaching cruise altitude. Because the aircraft had entered a very strong low-pressure area, there was a risk that the altimeter reading would be too high.

As the altimeter's needle passed through 2,000 feet, Boone eased back on the yoke and slowed the rate of decent. There were no breaks in the clouds. At an indicated altitude of 1,500 feet, Boone turned to Leveen and said, *"You win, Willie!"* The throttles were advanced and the plane began its reach for the stars. Passing through 19,000 feet, the crew donned their oxygen masks, but the passengers did not have that luxury. For them, the only option was an occasional draw on a small tube hooked up to the plane's oxygen system. As the plane passed through 20,000 feet, the limited amount of oxygen available to the passengers was useful only to keep them alive.

Perhaps it was better that their senses were dimmed. In the thin air, the C-54's rate of climb slowed. The plane could go no higher. It wallowed along between 25,000 and 26,000 feet. Leveen stood on the navigator's stool in the astrodome, looking for something to shoot with his octant.

Every time he exhaled, frost would coat the inside of the Plexiglas dome. Toward the east, Leveen noticed a pale white glow. Thinking it was more frost, he tried to rub it away, but the glow remained. Then it came to Leveen: the moon! Leveen took off his oxygen mask and raised the octant to his eye. Shouting at Boone to keep the plane level as possible, Leveen aimed the octant and pressed the button.

Several minutes passed before Leveen returned to his chart table, where he applied the readings from his octant to the sight-reduction tables. At first he thought the lack of oxygen had caused him to make a computational error, but he rechecked the figures several times and the answer came out the same each time: The plane and the 24 souls aboard were just off the coast of Norway.

Somehow, the tremendous head wind calculated many hours before had turned into an equally tremendous tail wind. *"Dan, do a 180!"* Leveen yelled. Trusting the navigator implicitly, Boone turned the aircraft to a southwesterly heading and began to descend. The engines were leaned to the maximum, and the propeller revolutions slowed as well.

Boone took the plane down to 500 feet, where occasional glimpses of whitecaps below were used to reset the airplane's altimeter. Boone then lowered the plane to 200 feet in order to minimize the head wind. By now, the flight was in peril. Boone turned to the flight engineer and gave the order: *"Prepare to ditch!"*

As the passengers put on their Mae West and the life jackets were readied for use, Leveen and Hoag continued to check radios but could not make any contacts. Almost 30 minutes went by before Boone exclaimed, *"Land!"* The ball was now back in the captain's court. His plan was to fly inland for 30 minutes, searching for an airfield or flat place on which to belly-land the airplane. If this failed, the plane would return to the coast and ditch as close as possible to shore. In reality, this option provided no more chance for survival than did a ditching in the open sea.

The allotted 30 minutes was rapidly running out when Hoag shouted: *"I've got Prestwick!"* It was 0430 GMT. The plane had been in the air for more than 12 hours and without a fix for 6.5 hours.

Hoag's fist beat a "QDL" into the code key, a request for a series of radio bearings. Then he held the key down for two minutes so that stations could orient their direction finding antennas toward the plane's signal. Shortly, Haag received a "QTF" (altitude and longitude) from Prestwick. He scribbled the figures on a scrap of paper and handed it to Leveen: 35"W, 53' 20"N. For the second time that night, Leveen turned toward Boone and yelled, *"Make a 180!"* The plane's position was near Colwyn Bay, Wales. Boone again complied without question. During the time since Boone had first sighted land (probably near Grimsby), the plane had flown across England and was on the verge of heading out over the Irish Sea. There was no chance of making Prestwick. The plane had to land—immediately!

Leveen's mind continued to work. From his days as a radio operator he remembered that the RAF had an emergency radio direction-finding system called "Darkee" to help disabled bombers find landing areas. He said later that he was praying to God when the frequency came into his head: 4220 kilocycles. He dialed in 4220 on the command set, keyed the microphone and called, *"Darkee! Darkee! Darkee!"* Out of the air came the reply: *"This is Darkee. Circle. Circle."*

Boone rolled the C-54 into a steep bank, picked up the 120-degree heading given by Darkee and reset the altimeter to the pressure provided. The plane was at 600 feet, but Darkee assured them that the highest obstruction in the area was "only" 400 feet. More vectors ensued as the plane worked its way toward the unseen landing area. Darkee finally radioed that the plane was directly above the airport, but the ground was still dark. Further instructions to descend to 500 feet, then 400 feet, and then 300 feet were complied with.

Darkee finally radioed that the airplane should circle to land. Even at 150 feet, no runway lights were visible. Boone asked for the airfield to shoot off a flare and a green arc appeared in the sky. He banked the aircraft sharply, causing engine Number 4 to sputter for lack of fuel. Boone feathered the prop and continued his approach. Suddenly, two rows of lights appeared through the windshield of the C-54. In all the excitement, Darkee had forgotten to turn on the runway lights!

Boone ordered the landing gear and flaps lowered and dove for the first of the lights. When the runway finally appeared, Boone firmly planted the wheels and then applied the brakes. As the far end of the runway came closer, he triggered the emergency braking system and locked the main wheels. When the plane came to a stop, Leveen noticed that engine Number 3 had also quit from lack of fuel.

The runway at the RAF fighter base was not very long, so the taxi back to the hardstand was quick. It was just as well, for the other two engines were suffering symptoms of fuel exhaustion as well. The local time was 0700 GMT, six hours past the ETA for Prestwick. The plane had been in the air for 15 hours. As the airplane came to a rest, Number 1 and 2 engines quit, out of fuel.

What happened to Boone, Leveen and company proves that sometimes you can do everything right but still be the victim of circumstances. Obviously, the cold front had moved in more quickly than predicted with winds stronger than anticipated. As for the radio problems, it seemed that Mother Nature had picked this moment in time to send forth a massive solar flare. The plane had actually flown over Prestwick and the radio signals had been heard on the ground. Repeated warnings from Prestwick that the flight was heading over the North Sea went unheard.

Oh, yes—one final note. The 18 passengers did arrive safely and went on to complete their duties. They were all U.S. Army generals returning from a conference in Washington. Had Willie Leveen not gotten his good moon shot and remembered the Darkee frequency, the Battle of the Bulge might well have had a different outcome.

MISSION WAS BERLIN

By Ellis H Murrey, Sergeant, Top Turret Gunner

On a Sunday morning in March 1944, we were awakened for a five o'clock briefing. At the briefing, when the map was uncovered, the route showed the mission of the day was Berlin.

Take-off was scheduled for 0800 hours and our bomb load was eighteen 100-pound and eight 500-pound bombs. We were due over the target at 1200 hours. At eight o'clock, we were rolling down the runway and into the air.

After maneuvering into the group formation, we headed across the English Channel and at 11:30 we began our approach to the target. Suddenly, the Number 1 engine started throwing oil from the cowl flaps. We continued on the bomb run and at 12 o'clock our bombs went hurling down on the target. After "bombs away", the pilot, 1st Lieutenant William H. Cocke Jr., attempted, but was unable, to feather the engine and it began windmilling and vibrating the plane pretty badly. At this point, the Number 2 engine started to lose power and the pilot ordered us to stand by to bail out if necessary.

By this time, the squadron had left us; the weather turned bad and visibility became poor. Since it would be impossible to make it to France, we ascended to 21,000 feet and headed due east for the Russian lines, dodging all the towns we could. Plenty of flak continued to plague us during our trip east.

At the Eastern Front, we were attacked by two fighters with Russian insignia. Our Number 3 engine caught fire and was feathered. We dived to put the fire out. At 7,000 feet we entered some clouds and prepared to bail out. We only had one engine, and were losing altitude fast. In the waist, preparing to bail out, I saw Sergeant William T. Martsch, the waist gunner, bleeding badly, and Sergeant Joseph J. Ryan, the ball turret gunner, sitting with his right arm just hanging. Sergeant Vincent O. Figini, the radio operator, advised the pilot, who told all to prepare for a crash landing.

Because of the crash, the plane broke in half at the waist. Since the plane was burning, we removed the wounded as soon as possible. Russian and Polish military were approaching the plane from all sides, and we showed them little American flags which convinced them we were Americans.

Polish farmers loaded the wounded on wagons and transported them to a hospital about two miles away. The rest of the crew walked or were driven to the hospital.

At the hospital, we were provided food and examined by a doctor. After examining the two wounded men, the doctor informed us via sign language that the waist gunner was dead and the ball turret gunner would have to have his arm amputated. Still by sign language, a nurse informed us that we were in Grodzisk, Poland, about 20 miles southeast of Poznan. We were advised that we would not be able to leave the hospital area for at least 10 days while the ball turret gunner healed.

The following day we conducted a funeral for Sgt. Martsch. The Russian commander must have ordered everyone in town to attend the funeral, as there was a crowd of about 2,000 people in attendance. A Polish priest conducted the service and Martsch was buried, with high honors from the Russians and the Poles, in the town square.

After a stay of about two weeks in Grodzisk, the ball turret gunner's arm was healed enough to travel, so we rode in a Model A Ford truck to Lodz, Poland, stopping overnight in Konn. In Lodz, we spent the night with some Americans from Poltovia, Russia, who were repairing a B-17 that had previously landed there. We spent the night with them, talking about our experiences and preparing letters to our families for them to take back and mail for us.

Since the Russians did not know if we were true Americans, we were taken to a barracks outside of town and placed under guard. Having a misunderstanding with the Russians, the men fixing the B-17 were also placed under guard in the barracks. We were kept under guard for about two weeks before we were finally taken to an airfield, loaded on a C-47 and flown to Kiev, Russia, where we were joined by about 75 other airmen who had been shot down.

We were still kept under guard, and every day we were told that we would be leaving that day. After several weeks in Kiev, we were loaded on trucks to take us to the Kiev train station for a train trip to

Odessa. Weather in Odessa was much warmer than in Kiev. After a short, one-night stay in Odessa, where we were allowed to shower and given clean underwear but not deloused, we were transported to an English ship in the harbor.

Learning we were in Odessa, the American Council in Odessa came to the ship and provided each person with a clean uniform and advanced pay of $10. After leaving Odessa and traveling about three days, we docked in Naples, Italy, and went to an American base about 20 miles outside of Naples. During our week's stay at the base, we visited Naples, saw Mount Vesuvius and visited the ruins of Pompeii. We were also issued more new uniform clothing. We left Naples on a little Italian boat for a week's trip to Marseille, France, and from there to Paris by train, which took about 24 hours. We were in Paris for about three days before departing for England and our base, from where we had taken off on March 18, 1945. We arrived back at the base on May 26th. It had taken us 5.5 hours to get to Berlin from Great Ashfield, but 70 days to get back to Great Ashfield.

A FAREWELL SALUTE

By Diane O'Day Cantor

On September 25, 1944, the Germans marched out of France as the country celebrated its liberation. Exactly 59 years to the day, Anita ("Anne" Lemonnier) Hartman, one of France's most decorated heroines for her work with the French Resistance during World War II, died at the age of 94.

On August 2, 1944, the nine members aboard the B-17 crew flying "Moonglow" were shot down over France. Three, including the pilot, were picked up by the Germans and sat out the rest of the war in a POW camp. The other five were MIA. Four of those men, including the bombardier, my father Edward F. O'Day, connected with the French Underground. They had seen the plane come down and so had the Germans, who were driving along the roads and searching the woods looking for crew members.

At this time, Mrs. Hartman was escorting downed airmen to safety. She collected my dad from the LeFerve home in Rambouillet and successfully delivered him to freedom on August 18th. He had flown his last mission. France would be liberated a week later. My father spoke about many of the dangerous circumstances they encountered, along the route, including several close calls involving the Gestapo or the SS. Despite the odds, she managed to deliver him safely to freedom, as she had done for so many other aviators who were fortunate enough to connect with the Underground.

Her background made her perfect for the job. She was a French woman raised in an English boarding school. She was disciplined and fluent in the languages most necessary for the work she would be doing. After the war, she married P.K. Hartman, a Naval Captain, moved to New York and lived a quiet, modest life, despite being the only member of the Resistance to receive the highest recognition possible by four countries. She was awarded the Medal of Freedom (United States), the Croix de Guerre (France), the King's Medal for Courage in the Cause of Freedom (England) and the Medal of Freedom with Bronze Palm (Canada). These awards recognized her disregard for personal safety while she hid, fed, sheltered and clothed the airmen. In addition, she procured medical attention and identification cards as necessary. She had also aided the airmen by escorting them from France by way of the Pyrenees Mountains to Spain. The honors bestowed recognized her work with several resistance groups, including Shelburne's Operation Bonaparte and the Comete Line.

She began her work with the Bourgogne line in November 1943. For this line, she and her mother hid airmen in their Paris apartment. The men whom they harbored were:

- 1st Lieutenant Elton Pete Hoyt III, Mentor, OH
  B-17 pilot
- 1st Lieutenant William Cook, Jr, El Paso, TX
  B-17 navigator
- Staff Sergeant Herbert Gebers, Holstein, IA
  Radio operator
- George Whitehead, Cambs, England
  RAF bomber pilot
- Harold Williams, Liverpool, England
  RAF Mosquito navigator
- Joseph Oliver, Brixton, London, England
  RAF Mosquito pilot

Through the Shelburne line they harbored:

- Staff Sergeant Robert K. Fruth, Smyrna, TN
- Harold Vines, West Fork, AR, gunner
- Stewart Barr, Philadelphia, PA, co-pilot
- Robert Sidders, Hastings, NE, assistant radio operator

During the course of her time with the Underground she personally escorted 32 men to safety, knowing that capture meant almost certain torture and death. She was very aware of this as she replaced Virginia D'Albert Lake, who had been captured.

The Germans picked Anita up and released her three times. During one interrogation, she could tell that the Austrian interpreter knew who she was, but did not betray her. It was just one of the moments of grace that allowed her to continue her work. Such other moments reported include an occasion when a hastily assembled German roadblock appeared at the end of a small street where she was leading three American flyers who did not have the customary forged document for ID. She was able to lead the men away without causing suspicion.

My father, who received the Distinguished Flying Cross for his efforts, never thought of and always dismissed any talk about his heroism. A word of such extraordinary weight, he would say, belongs to Anita Hartman. He says, *"It didn't take any courage to get shot down, but it did take a hell of a lot of courage for Anita Hartman to step into the fray, knowing the consequences she and her family could face if she were apprehended. She disregarded that danger."*

"The Germans had watched the plane go down, apprehended three members of the crew and were frantically searching for me. It wasn't me they wanted; they wanted her—she was the one with the information they needed to break the back of the Resistance."

He asked her why she was risking her life to save his. She told him, *"I had to do something or go mad."* She was recruited by the local grocer after expressing her distress for the Allies. She was told that if she really wanted to do something, come back in two days. The grocer would have two flyers for her to shelter.

Her mother, Madam LeMonnier, would take in the airmen and Anita would undertake the extremely dangerous task of interrogating the aviators before assigning housing to make sure they were not spies. In their desperation to crack the Resistance, the Germans were dropping English-speaking German soldiers from planes in order to infiltrate the operation.

She interviewed more than 60 aviators; she was then harboring many flyers including:

• Jim Kennedy, Canadian
• John Larkin, Thunderbolt pilot
• Russell J. Katz, B-17 co-pilot
• Edward F. O'Day, B-17 bombardier

Anita Harman leaves behind a remarkable legacy that touched many people, in many countries. She will be missed, but never forgotten. She will live on in the hearts and minds of those who are indebted to her. She would certainly dismiss such a notion, claiming that she only did what she needed to do at the time.

PIGGYBACK HERO

By Ralph Kenny Bennett, 100th Bomb Group

Recently, they laid the remains of Glen Rojohn in Pennsylvania's Greenock Cemetery. He was 81 years old, and looked like so many other WWII veterans whose names now appear in the obituary pages. Also like many of them, he seldom talked about those days. Oh, what a story he could have told. He won the Air Medal, the Distinguished Flying Cross, and the Purple Heart—all in one flight over Germany on December 31, 1944.

Captain Rojohn of the 100th Bomb Group was flying his B-17G Flying Fortress on a raid over Hamburg, braving heavy flak to drop their bombs. After the drop, the group turned back toward England, but were jumped by German fighters at 22,000 feet. The ME-109's attacked so close that Rojohn could see the faces of the German pilots. The group fought to remain in formation to take advantage of the combined guns of the bombers.

Rojohn saw a B-17 ahead of him burst into flames and fall downward. Gunning his ship forward to fill the gap, he felt a huge impact. His plane shuddered, felt very heavy and began losing altitude. Rojohn knew immediately that he had collided with another plane. A B-17 below him, piloted by Lieutenant William McNab, had slammed the top of his plane into the bottom of Rojohn's plane. McNab's top turret was now locked into the belly of Rojohn's plane, and Rojohn's ball turret had smashed into the top of McNab's plane. The two bombers were almost perfectly aligned—the tail of the lower plane was slightly to the left of Rojohn's tail section. They were stuck firmly together.

Three engines from McNab's plane were still running, as were all four of Rojohn's. McNab's fourth engine was on fire, with flames spreading back. The two planes were losing altitude. Gunning his engines, Rojohn tried to break free from the other plane, but to no avail. Fearing a fire, Rojohn rang the bailout bell for his crew to jump out.

McNab's ball turret gunner, Staff Sergeant Edward L. Woodhall Jr. had felt the collision impact and realized that he had no electrical or hydraulic power. Using the hand crank, he cranked the turret down until he could climb out and into the fuselage. He saw the ball turret of Rojohn's plane protruding through the fuselage of their plane with the turret gunner, Staff Sergeant Joseph Russo, hopelessly trapped.

Unaware that his voice was going out over the inter-com, Sgt. Russo started reciting his Hail Mary's.

In the cockpit, Rojohn and 2nd Lieutenant William G. Leek Jr. pulled back on the controls, trying to keep the plane from spinning into a dive and preventing the crew from bailing out.

Original Painting of the famous "Piggy Back" incident on December 31, 1944.

Struggling, the two turned the collision hybrid back toward the German coast. Since the crew could not jump from the bottom of the plane, he ordered them to work their way to the waist door and bail out.At this point, the plane below was aflame and fire poured over their left wing. Rojohn ordered Lt. Leek to bail out. Leek knew that without his help keeping the controls back, the plane would drop in a flaming spin and the centrifugal force would keep Rojohn from bailing out. Leek refused the order.

Meanwhile, the Germans on the ground thought they were seeing a new Allied weapon—an eight-engine double bomber. Anti-aircraft gunners had seen the collision and stopped firing, as the planes were unable to fight anymore. In the cockpit, Rojohn and Leek held the controls, trying to ride the falling rock. The two planes slammed into the ground. The McNab plane exploded, vaulting Rojohn's plane forward and upward. Slamming into the ground, the two planes slid forward and came to a stop. Rojohn and Leek were still in their seats. The nose of the plane was relatively intact, but from the wings back it was destroyed. Incredibly, neither pilot was badly injured.

Two of the six men who parachuted down from Rojohn's plane did not survive the jump; the other four, including the ball turret gunner, Woodhall, and, amazingly, four men from the other bomber, survived. All were taken prisoner. Several of them were interrogated at length by the enemy until they were satisfied that the Americans did not have a new secret weapon.

Rojohn did not talk much about his experiences and medals. Of Leek, he says, *"In all fairness to my co-pilot, he's the reason I'm alive today."* For 40 years he tried to track Leek down, and finally did in 1986. They had their first conversation since they shared that wild ride in the cockpit of their B-17. A year later, they were re-united at a 100th Bomb Group reunion in Long Beach, California. Bill Leek died the following year. Glenn Rojohn was the last survivor of that remarkable "piggyback" flight.

Jena, Germany: My Fifth Mission

By Roy Jillson

I will not lead you to believe that this was a rough ride today. We took a meager mauling compared to several of the other planes, however, for our tail gunner, Jim Eshelman, this proved to be a "Purple Heart" haul.

We did not go out looking for trouble; it just came up to meet us on this trip. Our primary target was Luskendorf, a railroad-marshaling yard, and we had a load of twelve 500-pound bombs. The target was to be bombed visually or not at all. My original crew had arrived in England in mid-February and we were assigned to the 385th Bomb Group at Great Ashfield as replacements. Many crews had finished their tours of 35 missions, and had earned the right to go home for a break before re-assignment. Furthermore, there were casualties requiring replacements.

The pilot of any nine-man B-17 crew is referred to as the "Aircraft Commander". He is the boss. Normally, in the military, there is a good bit of saluting and other examples of military courtesy; however, once a crew is formed, there is little of that, as each single member of a crew has a specific job to do. Each person serves to protect himself as well as every other person on board. There is this unspoken equalizer, ignorant of rank, at work among us at all times.

Pilots of new crews normally go on two bombing missions prior to flying with their crew on their first venture into combat. Our pilot, Bob Davis, flew his first mission to Kassel on the last day of February, just five days before. Upon his return, we met with him in his quarters for an informal visit and a debriefing of introduction to combat. His first trip was a relatively easy mission. Prior to the breakup of this meeting, he shared with us a package that he received from his wife in Illinois. As the non-airtight barracks at the base were only heated with pot-bellied stoves, she knew that the early months of any year in England can be penetratingly cold.

As a loving wife and concerned about her husband's comfort, she had knitted him an item of apparel designed to protect and cuddle his genitalia at any time, day or night. Since wartime patriotism prevailed throughout America, a certain color scheme was evident. The testicles were to be housed in a cup of blue kept in place by a cord tied with a bow, the shaft was white, and the crown was an appropriate red. He requested that we, his military family, not divulge his comforter to other personnel of the squadron. We thanked him for his "Show and Tell" and wished him well on his second mission scheduled for the next day. Little did we know that our co-pilot, Lt. Kim Crowe, would be asked the very next day to pack this knitted gift along with his other personal belongings to be sent home. Bob was killed on his second mission, along with 16 other men, in a mid-air collision just across the channel. The two planes, Armbruster and Ruseky, collided in dense clouds over Belgium. Of the 18 crew members, only a tail gunner, who rode down 15,000 feet in the tail of one of the planes, survived the collision.

Since our original crew was without a pilot, we were assigned to fill vacant positions in other crews. Today, March 19th, I was flying with Capt. Charles McCauley to the primary target, the railroad marshaling yards. On the cruise to "krautland", heavy clouds appeared below and since we were to bomb visually, the lead commander ordered our group to head for the secondary target at Jena and to bomb by instrument.

According to navigator Jack Shearman's calculations, we were to reach the bomb run's "IP" (Initial Point) at 1315. Receiving the checkpoint, messages were sent to Wing Headquarters at 1300. I signed off watch and went to the waist area to man the right waist 50-caliber machine gun. We were in a dangerous enemy fighter area.

We decided against donning our flak suits, trusting that the Germans would be inaccurate at scoring hits through the solid overcast. The entire crew was absorbed in looking out for ME-252 and 163 fighter jets, as well as the ME-109s and FW-190s. The contrails had formed solidly behind each plane, advertising our presence, and the Germans enjoyed attacking from out of the contrails and out of the sun.

Suddenly, the clouds evaporated and our target was dead ahead—24,000 feet below. We flew with lumbering vulnerability, bomb bay doors open, straight into heavy flak. Eighteen-year-old Eshelman in the tail said, *"Geez! Let's get the hell outta here!"* Level bursts of flak appeared not more than

20 feet from our fuselage. Devout words filled us as the sound and sight of black, dirty puffing explosions gave way to jagged fragments of red-hot steel, which sheared through the thin aluminum skin of our ship.

A minute before "bombs away", I hooked into my portable oxygen bottle and headed for the radio room and the open bomb bays. It was my duty to advise the bombardier and tell him whether or not all the eggs were out of the bays so that he would know if it was safe to close the bomb bay doors.

The bombs were clear, so I turned to head back to the waist gun. Krouse was unplugging himself and hurrying back to the tail section. While I was checking the bomb bays and off the interphone, Eshelman called out that some Jerry had hit him. I heard him say repeatedly, *"They got me, I'm hit! I'm hit!"*—a typical statement from a kid from Chicago. I filled my walk-around oxygen bottle, advised the pilot of my intended moves and headed back to the tail to help.

On the way back to the tail, I noticed several new holes in the waist position. On reaching the tail, I found Buck Krouse pulling Jim to the waist so we could care for him. Esh looked fairly well as he helped us drag him back to the waist. I gave both Buck and Jim spare oxygen bottles. Once in the waist, we placed a chute beneath Jim's head, got him into a comfortable position and plugged him into the waist oxygen supply. I headed for the radio room to advise the pilot we were all okay.

On this trip, we had a radar-jamming sergeant in the radio room who had been an ambulance attendant in civilian life. He realized that Esh needed additional help.

Cutting away Jim's clothing, we saw a rectangular flak wound just above Jim's left hip. I gave Jim a morphine shot and we took turns sprinkling plenty of sulfa powder into the wound and held compress bandages over it until his blood began to coagulate.

Esh complained of a lack of feeling from his waist down. Checking him over, we assured him that he had not been hit in any other place. The flak inside him caused considerable irritation but he was lying quietly.

We were still being pounded by flak and wide open to additional fighter attacks. Cooper, Flynn and Snowden were manning their gun turrets and keeping watch while we attended Jim. We realized that one of us should go back and man the tail guns. Since Krouse was manning his waist gun and keeping a close watch on Jim, I called Capt. McCauley and advised him I would take over the tail position.

From the flak-splattered tail position, I observed many of our fighters on a chase of the enemy. As we descended to 20,000 feet, we could see German artillery units battling our infantry down below. We could also see many fires among the ruins of well-remembered cities. Later, we reached areas flooded by the Germans. Entire farms, settlements and sections of land were under water. Normally, most sights are pretty, seen from the air. These were not. Bomb craters pitted the invasion beaches.

Captain McCauley called Jack Shearman, our navigator, and requested a course home north of the "Diver Gun Belt", a flak defensive system set up by the British to protect themselves from intruders and buzz bombs. Our planes identify themselves with IFF (identification, friend or foe) as they approach England; otherwise, they are considered enemy-manned aircraft and are shot down. Away from the formation, we went on our way home, crossing the channel into a real pea-soup fog.

We had come down below 10,000 feet and had no need for our oxygen masks. Some of us were munching on Hershey bars, while others were dragging on their first cigarette of the day. We had let down some more and were cruising over the water at about 250 feet. The swells and white caps of the bitter cold, choppy waters seemed to be lapping at Flynn as he spun around in his ball turret below us. A seabird bobbing on the water below knew better than to fly on a day like this.

As we neared the English coast, Capt. McCauley told us all to take a break. I had come forward from the tail and reached the radio room to request a coded weather report from our home base. Turning on the transmitter, I requested a QDM (magnetic course to steer with zero wind), and Shearman checked his course against this bearing.

Captain McCauley didn't like the sound of the base weather report; it was truly a lousy day to land an aircraft. Soon, we were within 20 minutes of the 385th base.

Captain McCauley and the co-pilot rounded the corners of the base-landing pattern, and Cooper fired the familiar red-red flares, signifying wounded aboard. When our wheels stopped rolling, the meat wagon was there to take Jim to the hospital. As we wished Jim well, we knew that he had flown his sixth and last mission as a valued member of our crew.

By Bill Varnedoe, Navigator

Crews in the 385th Bomb Group (H), 8th Air Force, stationed at Great Ashfield, England, were awakened for the 285th mission of the group on April 7, 1945. Like all crews of the group, Lieutenant George F. Burich and his crew arose, dressed and ate breakfast, as they had done for seven previous missions.

Lt. George E Burich and his B17 Crew

By now, the war was going very well and the Luftwaffe was all but non-existent. No great opposition was expected as the crews were briefed for a bombing mission to an enemy airfield at Güstrow, Germany. True, enemy anti-aircraft fire (flak) was just as intense as ever, if not worse, because all the 90mm anti-aircraft guns had, by now, been squeezed into Germany proper.

Following the briefing, the crews took off and assembled in scheduled formation for the mission. Although the group was flying at only 15,000 feet, a bit lower than their normal 23,000 feet, the flak was light and the mission went according to the briefed plan. It was a successful mission and the bombs hit the target.

As anticipated, there was no fighter opposition; the group turned from the target and took up a heading for home. Suddenly, a lone FW-109 was seen making a pass on the rear of the formation. Lt. Burich's B-17, Serial No. 448744, was positioned in the "Tail-end-Charlie" spot, the rear-most position in the group's formation. Both Sergeant Charles J. Stewart, the tail gunner in Lt. Burich's bomber, and Sergeant Leroy Lancaster, the tail gunner in Lieutenant Crow's plane, which was just ahead of Burich's B-17, spotted the FW-109 and started firing at it with their 50-caliber machine guns. Normally, a solo attacking enemy, once spotted and fired upon by our crews, would usually break off and prepare for another attack. However, this German pilot was different. He did not fire his guns at all, nor did he take any evasive action, but kept corning straight at the rear of Burich's B-17.

Contrary to instructions to fire only in short bursts, both Sgt. Stewart and Sgt. Lancaster locked down the triggers on their 50-caliber guns and kept firing at the incoming enemy plane. This did not deter the German at all. Without wavering, he kept his course coming directly at the Burich aircraft. Not changing his course, he impacted aircraft No. 44-8744 at the left wing root between engine Number 2 and the fuselage, and the impact tore the B-17's left wing completely off. In a moment, the B-17 disintegrated and the pieces fell to the ground.

No parachutes were seen by the other air crews in the group. Debriefing showed the aircraft as lost and the crew as MIA (Missing in Action). Missing Air Crew Report (MACR) No. 13721.

Far below on the ground, an American POW, William P. Marsicano, witnessed the ramming incident. He saw one parachute, which he thought emerged from a piece of the B-17, land over a hill nearby. This sighting is unusual because B-17 airmen normally did not wear a parachute, just the harness. After an incident like this, there is simply not time to find your parachute and attach it to the harness.

Shortly after the parachute and body were recovered, a German prison guard picked six American POWs, including Marsicano, to bury an American airman. At the burial site one of the POWs asked if he could pray over the body. He was given permission to do so, and found the body still warm.

At the site, the POWs found no parachute near the body and saw white skin on the finger and wrist of the body, which hinted at a missing ring and watch. Marsicano managed to remove and keep the airman's belt, which had the markings S3906, S for Stewart and 3906 for the last four digits of 33613906, Sgt. Stewart's serial number. Clearly, the body was Burich's tail gunner.

Based on the white skin markings, the POW burial detail concluded that this airman had parachuted safely but was subsequently killed and robbed by unknown assailants or by German soldiers.

Returning from the bombing mission, the 385th Bomb Group had no further problems and the remaining B-17s arrived safely back at Great Ashfield. Since Sgt. Lancaster's gun barrels had warped from the continuous firing, he was told that he was to be charged pay for new barrels. However, Lt. Charles Crow, his pilot, explained the ramming incident and Sgt. Lancaster did not have to pay for new gun barrels. Instead, he was given credit for killing the German pilot.

At that time, and for over 60 years, we all thought that the two tail gunners had killed the German pilot. We reasoned that the pilot did not shoot his guns at Burich's B-17 because he was dead, and we thought that the ramming of Burich's plane was a consequence of a dead man at the controls of the enemy plane. We did not believe that the German enemy was suicidal.

In the *Stars and Stripes* the next day, the front page showed a picture of a B-17 with its left wing off. The picture was taken on a mission on the 7th of April. I, Bill Varnedoe, navigator on Crow's crew, wrote the editor of the *Stars and Stripes* and requested a copy of the picture.

Without comment, the editor sent me an 8x10 glossy print, which I still have. Later, this photo was identified as that of another B-17. Although we think that type of collision and the date of the photo are striking, we believe that the photo is of the Burich ramming incident.

Sixty years later, in 2005, a shocking revelation came to light. On page 210 in Jane's "Battles with the Luftwaffe", there is a story by a German pilot named Walter Otto. He tells of how on that date (April 7, 1945), he deliberately rammed a B-17. He said that he carried no ammunition, hence the lack of firing during his attack. He said that he was thrown clear and parachuted to safety. Therefore, we now believe he must have been the parachuter the POWs saw. It neatly explained why no parachute was found on or near Stewart's body.

Later, we found that Walter Otto, in another report, said that he landed in Steinhuder Lake, which is about 60 miles away from the ramming incidence. Therefore, it is possible that the German pilot that rammed Burich will not have actually been Walter Otto, but someone else.

Like so many war stories, incidents that were positively considered accurate we later discover were reported incorrectly, causing confusion and, in some cases, even causing damage to our memories. It remains a fact, however, that Burich's aircraft of the 385th Bomb Group was rammed by an ME-109 and the crew was killed on April 7th, 1945.

385th Bomb Group

I would imagine that all of the aircrew members of the 385th Bomb Group have memories of certain missions that bring smiles to their faces and warm feelings to their hearts. Then there are those missions that they would just as soon forget about, but those memories keep coming back to haunt them in their dreams. This is a story about one of those missions that keeps coming back to haunt me. It was one of those "Big B" (Berlin) missions. I would bet that many "Big B" missions have come back to haunt many members of the 385th Bomb Group and the 8th Air Force. I know that this one certainly has for me.

First, I must tell you that I was a kind of an orphan in the 385th BG. On my last training mission here in the States, we had a fire aboard the ship and were forced to bail out at night over Nebraska. Many of the crew couldn't see the ground when they came down and were injured. I was one of the lucky ones to walk away from my landing. I was soon assigned to another crew and was headed overseas a few days after the crash.

My new crew arrived at the 385th BG about the time that one waist gunner was cut from each crew, and the radioman was assigned to come back and cover the open waist position during combat. As I was the last man to join the crew, I got booted so that a displaced waist gunner could take the ball and remain with the crew with whom he had trained. That left me flying with any crew that needed a ball turret gunner for the day.

I don't remember the exact date, but it was a mission in the summer of 1944. The mission started out with the normal routine. The night before we were told, *"You're flying tomorrow."* It was an early call the next morning and off to the mess hall, then on to the briefing room.

The officer in charge rolled back the screen covering the mission map and the lines on the map went out across the North Sea and then into Europe, all the way to Berlin. Moans and groans filled the briefing room, *"Not Berlin, again."* Then we headed for the hardstands to check everything out and get ready to fly.

The morning continued as usual, with preflight checks, taxi out and take off. We climbed to the pre-set altitude and got into formation. Then we headed out over the North Sea towards Denmark, but before reaching Denmark or the Helgoland Islands, we would make our turn inland for Germany. As we were doing this, the pilot reported that one engine wasn't performing up to par. Despite that, we were able to maintain our air speed, altitude, and stay in formation.

We made landfall and headed for "Big B". Not long after making landfall, we picked up some light flak, but it was enough, as one of our engines was hit. Now with one engine experiencing mechanical difficulties and another engine shot up, we started to fall behind the group, and we were losing altitude. You might say we were dropping like a rock. The bombardier came on the intercom to the pilot, *"Should I salvo the bomb load?"* The pilot came back, *"No! We are taking them to the target!"*

Well, any damned fool could see that at the rate we were dropping, by the time we reached Berlin, we would be on the rooftops! So, the bombardier salvoed the bomb loads anyway. The plane jumped as the bombs were released. The pilot immediately got on the intercom, *"You stupid, no-good son-of-a-BLEEP! What the BLEEP do you think you're doing?"*

I watched the bombs fall away from the ship until I lost sight of them, then I started watching the ground below for the impact. Far below, in a field near some buildings, a cloud of dust rose into the air. I often thought about that poor German farmer saying, *"What the hell did I do? Why are they bombing me?"*

The pilot continued with a steady stream of cussing and what he was going to do to the bombardier when we got back to base. The navigator broke into this tirade by giving the pilot a course heading and speed that would get us to Sweden. My thought was, *"Why not head southwest?"* Not too many miles that way and we would find the flight path of the groups that had already hit the target were using to go home. Although we couldn't keep up with the other bombers, there would be a good chance for a little fighter protection for us. As the argument continued onboard, we kept getting closer to "Big B".

We reached the outskirts of Berlin, out of formation and by ourselves. What did the pilot do? Instead of heading for Sweden, or trying to cross and catch our route home, he turns left and heads out around the east side of Berlin. There we were, all by ourselves in the BIG wild blue yonder, going around the east side of one of the most heavily defended cities in Germany!

I had the ball turret spinning round and round, looking for those German fighters that were sure to find us—and there they were, three of them, at six o'clock. I reported them over the intercom and began tracking them in my gun sights with my finger on the fire button. When they were about 1,000 yards and closing, I began to think that they might be P-51s, but I wasn't taking any chances. I was about ready to fire a warning burst in front of them when they racked up and showed their insignia; they were ours. They formed up and flew with us. I've always had the feeling that they were using us for bait, waiting for the Jerrys to jump us, but I was happy to see them!

They stayed with us the rest of the way around Berlin and until we got into the flight path of the groups heading for home. We finally made it back out over the North Sea on our way to England, but there was still one problem. All this time we had been running with two bad engines, and the pilot had been pouring the coal to the remaining two good engines to keep us going. Would those two engines hold up long enough to get us home? They did, but I heard later that the ground crew had to replace all four engines.

The enlisted crew went down to headquarters and told our story to anyone who would listen. We wanted off that pilot's crew before we were all killed. The answer we got was, *"Sorry, but we have to have all the crew in the air that we can get. You'll have to fly with him."*

I don't know what became of the rest of that enlisted crew. A few days later I was reassigned and put back on the crew with whom I flew overseas, and I finished my tour of duty with them. OH, HAPPY DAY! No more sightseeing tours around Berlin.

THE DEVASTATING MISSION TO BERLIN

By Oscar N. Winniford

Out of 26 missions that I flew, the mission to Berlin on October 6, 1944 was the most memorable to me.

On that day, under the command of Captain Robert Karin, our crew was scheduled to fly to Berlin. Just after departure from England, our oil pressure dropped in the Number 3 engine and we thought we would have to abort the mission. Luckily, the oil pressure rose back to an acceptable level and we were able to continue.

Although there was not much enemy action on the way to Berlin, we were advised by the high squadron that we had overshot the IP. As we approached the target area on the bomb run, we were slightly disoriented. The navigator told the crew, *"Look over to your left and you can see the coliseum where Jesse Owens won all his track medals."* We flew over Berlin and as we continued our flight, we saw many of our B-17s being shot down by enemy fighters. Berlin was being defended in the most brutal manner. The sight of our men going down was sickening; nonetheless, we kept on track.

During our bomb run, our Number 2 engine was hit by flak. The engine lost all 17 quarts of oil, which covered the whole left side of the fuselage. The pilot immediately called for crew check, starting with me, the tail gunner. Looking up, I saw that the sun was shining by the tail wheel

Tail Damage

through the vertical stabilizer. I spotted a large hole in the stabilizer and advised the captain that everything was not good. When he asked about the control cables, I replied that they had not been damaged. After a complete crew check, the pilot informed us that he could not feather the Number 2 engines, and that the prop was windmilling. He advised us that he would stay at high altitude.

Our radio operator, Richard Molzhan, was told to contact the air-sea rescue service, in the event we had to ditch the plane in the North Sea. He was answered with a "Stand by" from the rescue service. We stayed at high altitude until we visually saw England and our air base. Descending, we landed safely at the base.

Upon landing, we learned of the devastating loss of 11 of our aircraft on that mission. Our maintenance and other land crews were as shocked as we were. There were now 11 vacant hardstands.

An old infantryman once said, *"There are no atheists in a fox hole."* After this mission, I knew what he meant.

A Mission to Berlin, August 6ᵀᴴ, 1944

By Elmer Snow

You asked what it was like on a bombing mission to Berlin in 1944. Imagine you were in an eight-foot diameter aluminum cylinder five miles high with the temperature at 30-degrees below zero. The B-17 Flying Fortress you were in carried two tons of high explosives in the bomb bay, 1,000 gallons of 100-octane gasoline and 5,000 to 8,000 rounds of 50-caliber ammunition.

You were among a group of 1,000 planes flying in close formation on a bombing mission deep into Germany. At an altitude of five miles, the oxygen in the air was not adequate for breathing, so you breathed through a rubber mask attached to the oxygen supply by a flexible hose just long enough for movement about your gun position. You were in the upper turret.

You wore a heated suit and boots, a yellow flotation vest (called a Mae West) that would keep you afloat if your plane became damaged and went into the North Sea or English Channel, a parachute harness, a leather helmet with earphones, goggles and a throat microphone.

In case you were shot down and had to bail out over France, you had a pair of black civilian shoes tied to the parachute harness (the Germans could recognize downed airmen by their shoes or boots) and an escape kit containing European money and a photo of yourself in civilian clothes. These would aid the French Underground in preparing false identity papers for the attempt to escape capture. With the help of the valiant French Underground, many downed airmen walked out of France over the Pyrenees Mountains to Spain, where they could be repatriated.

Your mission to Berlin would be 10 hours long, at least seven of which were at high altitude on oxygen. As the bomber formation crossed the coast of Holland, enemy anti-aircraft fire (flak) was encountered. Oddly enough, the area you would cross in Holland was named Overflakkee Island.

Maybe you would get lucky and no one was shot down. You had to be more alert for enemy fighter attacks, which could occur at any time. As you continued your route to Berlin, you didn't have any fighter attacks, but other squadrons in the formation lost planes because of them.

Before long, you neared the target, "Big B", as it was nicknamed because of the heavy concentration of German flak guns. You could see the bursts of flak in the distance as you approached the point where you started the bomb run. The fiery black bursts of flak were all around you.

As you started the bomb run you were in the most vulnerable position because the bombardier was controlling the plane with the bombsight. The pilot and co-pilot had to maintain the altitude, air speed and a steady course until the "bombs away" signal from the bombardier. The five- to 10-minute bomb run seemed like it would never end. Fiery red bursts of flak burst very close and you flew through clouds of black smoke from the flak.

Inside the plane, it felt as if you were being hit with a giant sledgehammer. A close burst of flak sent fragments into the plane and a piece of flak came through the

Preparing to drop bomb load while taking on Flak

navigator's desk between his hands, breaking a navigation ruler he was holding. There were several other hits causing minor damage to the plane. The B-17 a hundred feet off your right wing took a hit and black smoke billowed out of the engine.

Within a few seconds you saw a door fly off the rear of that plane and a crewman bailed out. Almost as soon as he jumped he pulled the ripcord, his parachute opened and he floated down into Berlin. Your training was to free-fall to the cloud cover before pulling the ripcord to release the parachute. If no cloud cover was present, you were to delay opening the parachute for as long as possible. You weren't sure what was happening, but shortly afterwards the fire in the plane's engine went out and the bomber continued on with you to the target.

Later, you would often speculate what the fate of that lone individual was when he landed. Perhaps he died from lack of oxygen before he reached an altitude of 10,000 feet.

As soon as the bombs were away, the pilot took evasive action to avoid the flak. A slight change of course or altitude caused the flak to be inaccurate.

Before long, you were over the North Sea and you and the crew could relax. As you continued on a westerly course, the leader gave the signal for the formation to begin the gradual letdown from 25,000 feet to 5,000 feet, where you could remove your oxygen mask.

Strong headwinds on the North Sea reduced your speed from 150 mph air speed to 90 mph. It seemed to take forever to reach the coast of England. As you approached the coast, at 500 feet you got several rounds of flak from an English gun battery. No harm was done and your plane was quickly identified as an Allied plane. There was partial cloud cover over the air base, so your pilot searched for a hole in the clouds to let down. He landed the plane and you unloaded your guns, while a truck waited to take you and the rest of the crew to the briefing. Then, it was off to the mess hall for your first meal since breakfast at 6 am.

The last act of the day was to go to the armament shack to clean and oil the guns. Each gunner was responsible for his own guns. So ended your mission to Berlin. Perhaps you would be alerted again that night for another mission the next day...and so it was.

Now, imagine flying 35 missions with 285 hours of combat flying time. Some missions were easy—you called them "milk runs". All were very hazardous and you saw many bombers shot down over Europe. It was exciting but not fun; if it was fun they would call it FUN—not WAR!

The navigator was a native of Georgia and he had a southern drawl and a great sense of humor. He would always have some quip for the crew flying over Overflakkee Island when the German flak guns sent up their greetings. If it was a mission to Munich or other targets deep into the south of Germany you could see the Swiss Alps and he would always have a course plotted to get the crew to Switzerland if the plane should be damaged and not make it back to England.

THE LONG FLIGHT HOME

By Norman Lieb, 549th Squadron, 385th Bomb Group

I had completed my 27th mission on April 19, 1945 and was sent to the west coast of England for "R&R" (rest & relaxation). I was there on VE Day and was looking forward to returning to Great Ashfield. On my return, I was informed that I was being separated from the 385th, which was to return to the United States and then head on to the Pacific area.

Navigators who were considered to have completed their tour of duty were to be reassigned as navigators for the 9th AF A-26 bombers. The A-26 aircraft's crew consisted of only a pilot and an engineer and required a navigator for the flight to the States. I was happy that my tour of duty was ended and I would not have to go to the Pacific. The 385th left Great Ashfield while we waited for the A-26 aircraft.

We were briefed for our flight and took off from Great Ashfield. The last point of land was to be Scotland and then on to Iceland. I looked forward to this easy flight. The war was over and all we had to do was follow the radio beam.

We took off in stormy weather, reached the coast of Scotland and climbed above the clouds. We were flying along nicely, following the radio beam to Iceland, when about an hour or so into the flight, the radio went dead. The pilot and the engineer were not concerned, but being the navigator, I was.

I had to rely on dead reckoning and that meant using metro information that had been very unreliable on my missions. At some point, I would have to give the pilot an ETA for descent and I wondered what I would do if I did not see land when we broke through the clouds. When I gave the pilot the OK for descent, lo and behold, there was Iceland. I grabbed for my maps to do some pilotage, only to find all the lakes were unchartered. We continued and came over the base and made a routine landing with a very happy crew.

We stayed in Iceland for a week and then took off for the next leg to Greenland. We took off on a nice sunny day, but, once again, the radio went out. I was back to relying on dead reckoning, wondering what I would do if I didn't see land. I did see land, lots of land—big ugly-looking, barren mountains. I strained my eyes to the north and then to the south, and occasionally straight ahead. We were looking for a fjord, and there it was.

We waited there a week for good weather and finally took off for Labrador. It was a very pleasant flight—the radio beam took us right to the airfield, only my ETA was way off! The pilot and engineer made a few checks and determined that the air-speed indicator was not working properly. That meant the pilot would have to land by the seat of his pants, and I was sitting in the Plexiglas nose watching the runway speeding up, then a very bumpy undershot landing—but safe!

Our next leg was uneventful. We landed at Westover, Massachusetts, and in a few more days I was a civilian—home, safe and sound.

THE CARPETBAGGER

Courtesy of 385th Bomb Group

The 801st/492nd Bomb Group was an 8th Air Force Group known as the "Carpetbaggers". Their purpose was to fly "Special Operations" to deliver supplies to resistance efforts in occupied countries, to deliver specialized personnel to the area, and occasionally to bring back personnel from the field. The group flew out of Harrington, England, a secret OSS base.

Combat with the enemy was avoided, as it only endangered the success of the mission. Enemy anti-aircraft installations and detector posts were skirted as widely as possible to keep from revealing the presence or destination of the aircraft. To avoid any action with the enemy, flights were normally made at night and at low level. When it was necessary to cross enemy-held areas equipped with anti-aircraft defenses, the chosen route seldom exceeded 7,000 feet. Then, as soon the aircraft passed the dangerous area, it dropped down to 2,000 feet or lower. This made it more difficult to detect by sound or radar, since objects on the ground distorted the sound of a low-flying aircraft and radar had less time to pinpoint its location.

The majority of the Carpetbagger flights were made when the moon was out to make the ground visible to the navigator and bombardier. Non-moon flights were made using special navigation equipment known as "Rebecca", as well as S-phones and radio altimeters. However, the reception parties were required to have the ground counterparts of the Rebecca and S-phone equipment, and had to be able to use them expertly. Sometimes, bonfires were used if there were prominent landmarks that could be distinguished in the dark, such as rivers or lakes.

For more accurate drops, the aircraft flew at a speed of 150 mph or less within 400-600 feet of the ground. Personnel were normally dropped from a height of 600 feet, while containers and packages were dropped from heights of 300-500 feet.

Carpetbagger missions were flown with B-24D aircraft, since they were able to carry a bigger load and had a longer range than the B-17s. The aircraft were painted black and were specially modified for these clandestine missions. For exmple, there was no nose turret with 50-caliber machine guns because the bombardier and navigator required a clear view to see any signals from underground resistance so that supplies could be accurately dropped. The belly turret was removed and replaced with a plywood door so that OSS agents could jump.

Carpetbagger operations from England fell into two periods: January to September 1944, and from January 1945 until the last two months of the war in Europe. From January until September 1944, the USSAF delivered supplies to resistance groups in France, Denmark, Norway, Belgium and Holland.

Between January and September 1944, the 801st/492nd Bomb Group flew 2,263 missions, of which 1,577 (69%) were completed satisfactorily. Successful missions delivered 662 "Joes" (agents), 18,535 containers with supplies, 8,050 "Nickels" (bundles of propaganda leaflets), 10,725 smaller packages of supplies, 26 pigeons (for messages, not eating), and 437 passengers to occupied Europe.

Carpetbagger Mission

385th Bomb Group

The Air Corps had 28,000 men killed in action, more than any other branch, percentage-wise. Twenty six-thousand of these were in the 8th Army Air Corps. There was a 75-percent chance you wouldn't finish your assigned missions. Not good.

Numbers never seem to add up, but according to the 385th Bomb Group's records, they had 1,452 men complete their tours. 442 were Missing in Action, 231 Killed in Action, 458 became POWs, 13 were interned by neutral countries, and 252 evaded capture after being shot down and returned to England. This adds to a grand total of 2,848 men who flew missions in the 385th Bomb Group. Part of the difference in numbers is explained by many facts. Men reported missing were sometimes killed in action. Some men escaped from a crash landing after bailing out and AFTER they had been reported killed or missing. In short, you could only guess at the fate of the airman until it was confirmed, which might be in years—or not at all.

Adding in the "Paddle Feet" (ground personnel), all told, there were an estimated 3,000 men at Great Ashfield in World War II. There were 32 bomb groups in the 8th Air Corps. The whole 8th Air Force had 350,000 soldiers; 200,000 were in combat crews.

Post-war statistics show casualty numbers for World War II were 0.88% for the Navy, 2.08% for the Army (as a whole), 2.94% for the Marines, 7.42% for the Army Air Corps (as a whole), and 27% for Air Force air crews!

The average crewman was overseas in the 8th Air Corps about six months. By then, he would have completed his tour or become a casualty.

The 385th had a total of 430 B-17s serve the group. The average B-17 only lasted about six months before being either shot down or being so badly damaged that it had to be scrapped. On average, there were about 40 to 60 operational B-17s at Great Ashfield at any one time.

The 385th sends a present to Hitler at Christmas

The 100th Bomb Group was famous for being singled out by the Luftwaffe as a highly desirable target. After being shot up on a mission, one of the bombers from the 100th was straggling and was intercepted by a German fighter. The fighter gave him the "Wheels Down" signal, which told him to follow and land. The bomber obeyed and began to follow him, but once they got over the German base, the bomber opened fire, knowing that the German fighter was probably low on fuel. The bomber got away and made it back to England, but the 100th paid a big price. The *Luftwaffe* would actually instruct their fighters to pass up some formations of the bombing force, only to look for and open fire on those belonging to the 100th Bomb Group.

WON'T BE LONG BEFORE THEY WILL GONE

By Captain Stephen R Ellison, MD
Provided by the 385th Bomb Group

I am a doctor specializing in Emergency Medicine in the Emergency Departments of the only two military Level One-Trauma Centers. They are both in San Antonio, Texas, and care for both civilian and military personnel emergencies. San Antonio has the largest military retiree population in the world, because of the location of these two big military medical centers. As a military doctor training in my specialty, I work long hours and the pay is less than glamorous.

One tends to become jaded by the long hours, lack of sleep, food, and family contact, and the endless parade of human suffering. The arrival of another ambulance does not mean more pay, only more work.

Most often, it arrives with a victim from a motor vehicle crash, or it could be a person of dubious character who has been shot or stabbed. With our large military retiree population, it is also likely to be a nursing home patient. Even with my enlisted service and minimal combat experience in Panama prior to medical school, I have caught myself groaning when the ambulance brought in yet another sick elderly person from one of the local retirement centers that cater to military retirees.

I had not stopped to think of what citizens of this age group represented until I saw "Saving Private Ryan". I was deeply moved— not so much be the carnage in the first 30 minutes of the film, but by the sacrifices of so many. I was touched most by the scene of the elderly survivor at the graveside, asking his wife if he'd been a good man. I realized that I had seen these same men and women coming through my Emergency Department, and had not realized what magnificent sacrifices they had made. The things that they did for me and everyone else that has lived on this planet since the end of that conflict are priceless. Situation permitting, I now try to ask my patients about their experiences. Like many who served in WWII, Korea and Vietnam, they don't talk about their experiences. In fact, most would never bring up the subject without an inquiry. I have been privileged to an amazing array of experiences, recounted in the brief minutes allowed in an Emergency Department encounter.

These experiences have revealed the incredible individuals I have had the honor of serving in a medical capacity, many on their last admission to a hospital.

There was a frail elderly woman who reassured a young enlisted medic who was trying to start an IV line in her arm. She was what we call a "Hard Stick" (hard to find a vein). She remained calm and poised, despite her illness and the multiple needle-sticks into her frail veins. As the medic attempted again to find a vein, I noticed a number tattooed across her forearm. I touched it with one finger and looked into her eyes. She simply said *"Auschwitz"*. Many later generations would have loudly and openly berated the young medic in his many attempts. How different was the response from this person who'd seen unspeakable suffering.

Another incredible individual was a long-retired colonel who as a young officer had parachuted from his burning plane over a Pacific island held by the Japanese. Now an octogenarian, he had cut his head falling at home, where he lived alone. Unfortunately, due to the usual parade of priority ambulance patients, it was well after midnight before the staff performed a CT scan and sutured his wound. Of course, still spry for his age, he asked to use the phone to call a taxi to take him home. However, in his haste to get to the hospital he had left his wallet at home. He then asked if he could use the phone to make a call to his daughter, who lived just seven miles away. We looked at each other and with great pride told him he could not use the phone, because he had done enough in the service of our country; the least we could do was to get him a taxi home. We were also honored to pay for it ourselves. My only regret was that my shift didn't end for several hours, so I was not able to drive him myself.

I was on duty the night Master Sergeant Roy Benavidez came through the Emergency Department for the last time. He was very sick. I was not the doctor taking care of him, but I walked to his bedside and took his hand and remained silent. He was so sick that he didn't know I was there. I'd read his Congressional Medal of Honor citation and wanted to shake his hand. Unfortunately, he died a few days later.

I remember many other gentlemen I came to admire on my shifts. One served with Merrill's Marauders, another was a survivor of the Bataan Death March, still another was a survivor of Omaha Beach, there was a 101-year-old WWI veteran, a former POW who was held in frozen North Korea, the former Special Forces medic with non-operable liver cancer, and the former Viet Nam Corps Commander. Yes, I remember them all.

Sure, I may still groan when yet another ambulance comes in, but now I am much more attentive of what an honor it is for me to serve these precious men and women.

It is sad that I have watched our Congress turn their back on many of these individuals who've sacrificed so much to protect our liberty. I am also observing later generations that appear selfishly engrossed in abusing those liberties. I might add that we enjoy those liberties because they paid the ultimate price for us. For that reason, it has become my personal endeavor to encourage our nurses and young enlisted medics to embrace these amazing individuals as they encounter them in our Emergency Department.

Slowly, our staff is becoming more aware and appreciative of how incredible these men and women are, and the important part they played in our history. They are hearing the stories of sacrifice that provided the very freedoms they enjoy—and have so easily taken for granted. Thus, seeing the staff's response to these particular citizens has made me think that perhaps all is not lost in the subsequent generations.

My experiences sure have solidified my belief that we are losing an incredible generation, and this nation doesn't realize the value of what it is losing. For those in our government who seem not to care and for our civilian populace that just want a hand out, take note. These men and women know what it means to "earn" freedom, and they walk in that freedom proudly as a result. We would do well to remember that we, too, must "earn" our freedom and our right to be associated with these heroes of the "Greatest Generation".

AFTER WORDS

"*D*an *Harding, bomber pilot*", I thought. *"Big deal."* The memories of combat flying in the 8th Air Corps have stayed with me my whole life, some of them pleasant and some very horrifying. I've wondered a thousand times what I might have done different. I don't know what, but something. Over the years I've dreamed about the crash. In one dream I landed the 088 on its back and everyone aboard was killed. In another dream I only lost half the crew. However, I can tell you this, not once in any of my dreams did the ball turret gunner fail to survive. I'm sure he looks down on me with grace, but the memory still haunts me to this day.

I'm 88 years of age and still question whether we used the right judgment. *"Could we have landed the plane differently? Did we exhaust all alternatives?"* I agonize over the memory—who wouldn't? I continue to be extremely sorrowful at the decisions many of us had to make during the war. I sure didn't expect to have to live with those decisions for the next 65 years.

Times were tough in the pre-war years. My father worked on road construction with the "Works Progress Administration", an idea by President Roosevelt. His pay was a dollar a day plus some corn flour to make bread every now and then. As I look back, I think it was the poverty prevalent during those times that led Dad to drink. After all, drinking was very much in style in the late-'30s. Everyone was very poor in those days. No one had a car, no one ever took a vacation, the main source of entertainment was family "get-togethers" or an occasional picnic.

In spite of all the hardships, when the call came, my friends and I joined up and went to war. We won that war because of the concerted effort of the generation living at the time. I am not talking about only the military; I'm including the great effort that was made on the home front. People at home took up the fight by taking jobs in our factories. The tremendous manufacturing capability was the glue that made it all work.

Eight million Americans were trained in skilled positions by the War Department. The unselfish support on the home front was the primary reason for our success. Victory in Europe was due to our nation's patriotism, devotion and determination.

Many women got the toughest jobs and did them well; the war could not have been won without the women. "Rosie the Riveter" represented the women who lent their delicate handywork for manufacturing of planes, ships and armaments (Rosie became an iconic figure depicting the many women who went to work in our factories). In contrast to today, women were the most patriotic. They were willing to support the troops and be satisfied with the role they had been dealt. They didn't need to be any part of the suffering and dying, and they shouldn't have been.

"Rosie the Riveter" color poster by J. Howard Miller

Many people I speak with from that generation are concerned at the cost of today's Middle Eastern war. It costs twice as much to wage, even in yesterday's dollars, because we have to be so careful to provide for our soldiers going to combat—and rightfully so. However, with women entering battle, now we have to consider things like maintaining stocks of baby food, diapers, face creams, lotions, hair curlers or whatever in our PXs and BXs around the world. Medical units must not only think of combat wounds, but pregnancies, mammograms, vaginal problems, and other things common to females and children. We must have a staff of gynecologists on base. I could remember when going to the PX was the place you got cigarettes, shaving cream, and toothpaste— what a difference from today's military!

I find my thoughts drifting about this current plight. What do we get for all this? Nothing more than a "Politically Correct" military. Who is commissioned with raising our young? Like it or not, our young people will be the next generation of warriors. Oh, sure...many women can handle the load. After all, they're a tough bunch. It just seems to me we are being deceived by confusing the roles. Guess I embrace the school of thought that says a real man will shield women from battle and respect their role in the community.

Think about it—with women in battle, do we kill more of the enemy? Are there more villages liberated? I challenge that not one less American casualty will be reported. However, the stern reality is a greater strain on our healthcare system. The Veterans Hospitals get a 50% increase in patients...long-term. But the most damage is done in our communities at home. With women in combat, who is left with the task of raising our young? Shouldn't this be a far more admirable challenge than firing a weapon?

Where will this eventually lead? The first problem we might have with subsequent generations would be getting them into a uniform at all. They might be inclined to embrace a wave of thought that says, "Who are they to tell me to serve?" Potential recruits might be inclined to insist on the freedom to appear as they wish, wearing pelvic-fitting trousers, tank tops, tattoos, body piercings and Mohawk haircuts. After all, isn't that within our civil rights, or so they might claim.

Don't get me wrong. All in all, our current generation of Americans is a wonderful group of young people. They are smarter, bigger and stronger than the WWII model, but are there enough of them? The question concerns me. I wonder what would happen if the United States was attacked on our home front and we had to rally the masses. Would there be enough young men and women loyal to our country?

In many ways our country has made giant strides. We have beautiful homes, wonderful cars, and products we never dreamed of before WWII. We have travel available to us that would have been unimaginable then. We do not, however, have the same type of friendships, camaraderie or social functions that were so important to us in the past. We don't have the close-knit family. A mother might have a child in New Jersey, another one in China (and one who knows where). In the past, if you wanted to speak to your son, you only had to go down to the barn and you'd find him milking the cow.

I've spent many hours alone, thinking about our current predicament. My thoughts drift to all the boys who didn't come home after the war. Many stories come to mind, each of them catastrophic, each of them human, and each of them heroic. Over the years I have been strengthened by frequent visits to the Veterans Hospital, where I meet new friends...friends with whom I have a lot in common.

There are also the annual meetings I participate in with my old bomb group. These have helped me cope. I've stayed close to my wartime buddies over the years but, sadly, at every meeting the discussion inevitably turns to who has died and who is still alive. Of course, the memories related to those I served with will forever be stored in my private memory bank. I garner strength from those memories. Those memories have helped me fight the scars of loneliness and despair that war indelibly leaves on your soul.

D an Harding Senior has been retired from the U.S. Air Force for many years. Those years have given him plenty of time to think about what has transpired since his 25 years of service. He was happily married for 41 years before losing his wife to cancer. He has three wonderful children, now in their 40s and 50s, who have all led happy and successful lives.

His oldest son, Dan Junior, is a geologist and has traveled all over the world for a major oil company. Dan Junior has since retired, but lives in the same town as his father. Dan Senior also has two daughters, both married, and he is the proud grandfather of three boys and three girls.

Things were so different when he was young. The world was in turmoil, but the "Greatest Generation" was there to answer the call. They defended the country without hesitation and with honor. Sure, there was fear. Everyone knew the German military forces were the best in the world. They had the largest standing Army, Navy and Air Force on the planet. Then you throw in Italy and Japan and you're talking about real power and a seemingly insurmountable force. They were known as the Axis of Power.

The Axis forces had the best weaponry, including radar, jet aircraft, rockets and the famous "Buzz Bomb" that nearly destroyed London. Germany, as well as Japan, had suicide bombers; in Germany, they called them the *Rammkommando*.

While we were flying P-40s, the Germans had a pure jet fighter and a flying stealth fighter-bomber. The Japanese had the largest and most modern navy, with aircraft carriers and battle ships. Their military men had the will to fight to the death for their country. No, it didn't look good in 1941, not good at all. We had no army to speak of, and had just lost half our active navy at Pearl Harbor. Not to mention that we had no modern aircraft at the time. In fact, our "Air Service" was considered the "red-headed stepchild" by most of the military.

Today, we have wonderful military forces, but would it be enough without depending on the people to get behind an all-out war effort? Is our population ready for this? Are we dedicated to ourselves so strongly that we wouldn't dedicate ourselves to our country? Could we mobilize our industry? Could we even get it back from China? If our current slate of politicians and big business had anything to say about it, I doubt we could.

From Dan's perspective, nothing could compare with our effort during WWII. He and others from that generation shuddered at the pictures of Jane Fonda manning a North Vietnamese anti-aircraft gun during the Vietnam War. They would love to have asked Henry, her father, how it made him feel. It must have hurt him terribly, considering he was a solid patriot and an icon for our youth to follow during WWII.

One dearly remembered aviator was the former coach of the Dallas Cowboys, Tom Landry. Coach Landry took time out from his studies to serve in the Air Corps during WWII. In 1944 he was commissioned as a Second Lieutenant and assigned to the 493d Bombardment Group at RAF Debach, England, where he was the co-pilot on a B-17 Flying Fortress. Coach Landry completed a combat tour of thirty missions and was the survivor of a crash landing in Belgium.

In contrast to today's passive climate in Hollywood, many film stars in the Hollywood community back then joined the military, and many of them saw combat. Clark Gable flew six missions with the 351st Bomb Group. He was the brightest star in Hollywood, but he dropped his acting career, joined up, went through officer training and went into combat. He was a great help to morale, as well as the war effort.

Clark Gable with 8th AF B-17F with pre-Cheyenne tail position, in Britain, 1943

Hunsberger
Clark Gable with 508BS CO, Keith Birlem—Photo taken at Peterborough   49

Major James Stewart

Jimmy Stewart, of the 445th Bomb Group, participated in at least 10 missions and was awarded the Air Medal. Jimmy rose to the rank of Brigadier General in the USAF Reserves. He was another patriot that we could be proud of.

Andy Rooney, of "60 Minutes" fame, flew a mission with the 385th Bomb Group aboard the "Lady Liz". He later co-wrote a book titled "Air Gunner" about his experience and others.

Andy Rooney accompanied American crews on bombing missions over Europe.

Naming our airplanes was the sport of the day in the 8th Air Corps. It was a contest to see who could paint the sexiest picture, think up the cleverest name and paint the most "bombs" on the fuselage (indicating number of missions flown and swastikas for the number of enemy aircraft destroyed).

Today, protesters would scream bloody hell and demand we paint over those images, citing "sexism" or "discrimination". However, the men from the WWII generation will tell you, *"The women of our generation wanted a man to be a man. They respected the fact that we were ready to stand tall and fight for their freedom. They loved their boys in uniform."*

Shack Bunny, Sack Time, The Vibrant Virgin, and Stormy Angel – B-17 Nose Art

Yes, one wonders today if we could count on the likes of our major universities to help with ROTC training, recruiting, etc. Couldn't our country get along without some churches protesting our dead soldiers? Of course, we shouldn't tread on constitutional rights, even if it might mean losing our modern day wars.

But "fear no evil"...the men and women from the "Greatest Generation" stepped up and won the war they were faced with in the 1940s, preserving the freedom and liberty we enjoy today. Just as our marvelous young people who choose a military career would do today. We remain firm believers that the values of our country will continue to exist as long as they are entrusted to the hands of our wonderful airmen, soldiers, sailors and marines.

APPENDIX

Charles D. Hamlin, of Rockland, Maine, has a long history of military experience. In 1942, at the age of 15, he left his home and small town to join the U.S. Army. He was assigned to Radio School and Gunnery School, and successfully completed both. In 1944 alone, he flew 35 missions in the 8th Army Air Corps, mostly as a ball turret gunner. He celebrated his 17th birthday on a mission to Germany.

He remained in the military for 20 years, retiring at the ripe old age of 36 with a whopping pension of $145 a month. His military career included nine years of U.S. embassy duty with service in Mexico, India, and Egypt, along with four years in NATO service in Turkey.

Married to a former Miss Egypt and movie personality from Cairo, Mona, Charles has enjoyed 55 years of wedded bliss so far. They currently live in Houston and have two children, Joseph and Jaqueline, and five grandchildren.

His many missions included most of the missions described in this book, such as the four Berlin missions, Augsburg, Munich, Stettin, Poland, Hamm, Zwickau, Leipzig and Regensburg. There were others where B-17s would fly into known German fighter zones, without carrying bombs, to find and destroy enemy fighter aircraft. These missions carried only proven gunners who had shot down at least one enemy aircraft.

E. N. White Crew - Charles "Chuck" Hamlin kneeling front center

Sgt. Charles "Chuck" Hamlin's Escape Kit Photo

In Memoradum

The Author has often wondered if our current generation would measure up to the men and women who served in WWII—if they could possibly compare to patriots like his brother, Oliver, who died on a rescue mission in the northern Atlantic Ocean. Oliver enlisted in the U.S. Army on December 8, 1941, one of millions who answered the call.

Oliver applied for and received an assignment to pilot training but, unfortunately, an illness during his training prevented him from graduating. He applied for crew training as a radio operator and in deference to his religious beliefs, requested assignment to an organization that was in the business of saving rather than taking lives. Oliver was granted that request and assigned to an Air Sea Rescue unit in Santa Maria, Azores. There, he crewed on a PBY, an amphibious twin-engine aircraft that landed on the ocean to pick up survivors who had ditched their planes.

In September 1945 Oliver, his crew, and an unknown number of people they were rescuing apparently drowned. They simply disappeared. No funerals, no memorials, no name tracing...only empty graves in North Africa. It was reported that the PBY was overloaded in its attempt to rescue all the survivors and crashed on take-off.

To Oliver's family, he had disappeared from the Earth, never to be seen or heard from again. They were left with a flag, a certificate and an empty lifetime of not knowing for sure what had actually happened. The family only knew that he was gone; the only remaining evidence that he had ever been here was a little church that Oliver and some friends had built on that lonely island far out in the northern Atlantic Ocean.

Oliver left behind some big shoes to fill, but his family knows that somehow our country always pulls together and rises to the occasion.

Photo Credits

COVER: Cover provided by Hadeon Design Studios

Page 10
1. Great Ashfield (Source: Public Domain)
2. Original sign hanging at the Great Ashfield Airdrome in England (Source: Public Domain)

Page 11
3. HO-229 German Stealth Fighter-Bomber (Source: USAAF Photo - Public Domain)

Page 12
4. Cover of LIFE Magazine featuring the Mighty 8th on July 26, 1943 (Source: LIFE Magazine)

Page 13
5. B-17 "Flying Fortress: (Source: USAAF Photo - Public Domain)
6. B17 - Latest Rumor (Source: Mighty 8th Air Force Museum, Pooler, GA)

Page 14
7. Flying Through Flak (Source: USAAF Photo - Public Domain)

Page 18
8. (Source: Pilot Training Manual for the B-17 Flying Fortress)

Page 28
9. (Source: Pilot Training Manual for the B-17 Flying Fortress)
10. Tail Gunner Position (Source: USAAF Photo - Public Domain)

Page 29
11. Top Turret Gunner Position (Source: USAAF Photo - Public Domain)
12. Ball Turret Gunner Postion (Source: Unknown)
13. Ball Turret (Source: USAAF Photo - Public Domain)

Page 34
14. Picture of Hedy Lamarr painted on the nose of "Heavenly Body" (Source: W.W. Varnedoe, Jr.)

Page 37
15. Replica of Captain Glenn Miller's downed plane. (Source: National Museum of the USAF)
16. Captain Glenn Miller (Source: USAAF Photo - Public Domain)

Page 39
17. 1st Lt. Lawrence DeLancey's crippled B-17 (Source: USAAF Photo - Public Domain)

Page 41
18. British Pathfinder Mosquitoes (Source: Royal Air Force)

Page 43
19. Right photo:German Messerschmitt Me-262- First Jet Fighter in operational service (Source: Public Domain)
20. Left photo:Messerschmitt Me163A Rocket Interceptor (Source: Royal Aeronautical Society)

Page 46
21. Map of Germany printed on Silk (Source: Waddington Archive)
22. Monopoly Game Box Top (Source: www.military-times.co.uk)

Page 47
23. Top Secret Document Authorizing Waddington Monopoly Games (Source: Public Domain)

Page 48
24. Left Photo: Goldfish Club Membership Card
25. Right Photo: Arm patch for Goldfish Club
(Source: Both photos provided by Goldfish member Lt. Col. Eddie Deerfield & the 303rd Bomb Group Association - www.303rdbg.com)

Page 52
26. Lined up ready for take off (Source: USAAF Photo - Public Domain)

Page 60
27. Dropping Bombs (Source: Mighty 8th Air Force Museum, Pooler, GA)

Photo Credits

Page 61
28. Front Toggelier/Gunner Position (Source: National Museum of the United States Air Force)

Page 62
29. Bomb Salvo (Source: Mighty 8th Air Force Museum, Pooler, GA)

Page 64
30. P-51 Escort (Source: Wikimedia.org)

Page 66
31. Lt. Col. Bruce W. Carr, Union Springs, NY, stands by "Angels Playmate", he had claimed 22½ aerial victories by the end of WWII (Source: 354th Fighter Group)

Page 67
32. AT-6 Trainer (Source: Encyclopedia Britannica)
33. Flying-tiger-p-40 (Source: Public Domain)
34. Angels' Playmate (Source: Public Domain)

Page 71
35. Bruce Carr's stolen F-190 (Source: USSAF Public Domain)

Page 76
36. German Focke-Wulf-190 (Source: Public Domain)
37. German ME-109s in flight (Source: Public Domain)

Page 80
38. P-51 Bomber Escort (Source: Mighty 8th Air Force Museum, Pooler, GA)

Page 86
39. "Rum Dum" (Source: 385th Bomb Group)

Page 88
40. "Rum Dum" Nose Damage (Source: 385th Bomb Group)

Page 105
41. Original Painting of the famous "Piggy Back" incident on December 31, 1944. (Source: Unknown)

Page 111
42. Lt. George E Burich and his B17 Crew (Source: George Burich Jr.)

Page 117
43. Tail Damage (Source: Public Domain)

Page 120
44. Preparing to drop bomb load while taking on Flak (Source: 385th Bomb Group)

Page 125
45. Carpetbagger Mission (Source: David Arnett with the 492ndbombgroup.com)

Page 127
46. The 385th sends a present to Hitler at Christmas (Source: 385th Bomb Group)

Page 133
47. "Rosie the Riveter" color poster by J. Howard Miller (Source: U.S. National Archives)

Page 137
48. Clark Gable (Source: Public Domain)
49. Clark Gable with 8th AF B-17F with pre-Cheyenne tail position, in Britain, 1943 (Source: Public Domain)

Page 138
50. Major James Stewart (Source: National Museum of the USAFF)
51. Andy Rooney accompanied American crews on bombing missions over Europe. (Source: unknown)
52. Shack Bunny (Source: 385th Bomb Group)
53. "Sack Time" (Source: 385th Bomb Group)
54. The Vibrant Virgin (Source: 385th Bomb Group)
55. Stormy Angel (Source: 385th Bomb Group)

Page 143
56. E. N. White Crew - Charles "Chuck" Hamlin kneeling front center (Source: 385th Bomb Group)
57. Sgt. Charles "Chuck" Hamlin's Escape Kit Photo (Source: Author Charles D. Hamlin)

GLOSSARY OF TERMS

A-26	Medium U.S. bomber
Bail out	Parachute from the aircraft
Ball turret	Gun turret in the belly of the aircraft
B-17	Flying Fortress aircraft
B-24	Liberator aircraft
Bomb runs	Course to steer from Initial Point to target
Bought the farm	Died
Buncher	Beacon at each base to assist aircraft in forming
Buzz bomb	German jet-propelled flying bomb
C-47	U.S. transport aircraft
C-54	U.S. transport aircraft
Chaff	Aluminum foil strips to confuse German radar
Coast out	Departure point from England
Cowling	Engine covering
C.O.	Commanding officer
Contrails	Vapor trails streaming from aircraft at high altitude
Crash-land	Wheels-up landing
Darkee	British radio station for navigation aid and ID
Ditch	Land in water
ETA	Estimated time of arrival
Flugzeugabwehrkanone	German word for anti-aircraft gun
Feather a propeller	Adjust the propeller blades to neutral
FW-190	German fighter aircraft
Flak	Anti-aircraft shell exploding
Flak suit	Armored jacket
Geezer	English gas water heater
GMT	Greenwich Mean Time, time in London

GLOSSARY OF TERMS

Go around	Not landing on the first approach to the runway
Goldfish club	Airmen who have survived landing on water
Halifax	British heavy bomber
Hardlife	Radio call sign of base control tower
Hardstand	Concrete parking stands located around the perimeters of an airfield in order to disperse the aircraft
Heated suit	Electric high altitude flying suit
IFF	Identification system installed in aircraft
IP	Initial Point; beginning of bomb run
Jerry	Nickname for German troops
Kraut	Nickname for Germans
Krautland	Nickname for Germany
Lancaster	British heavy bomber
Lucky Bastard Club	Certificate for completing all assigned missions
Lyon's Corner House	Popular restaurant in London
LF	Low Frequency Radio
LOP	Line of Position
Luftwaffe	German Air Force
Lorry	British for truck
MACR	Missing Air Crew Report
Mae West	Life jacket
Marshalling yard	Railroad yard
ME 109	German fighter aircraft
ME 262	German jet fighter aircraft
ME 163	German jet fighter aircraft
Mighty Eighth	U.S. 8th Army Air Corps
Mohawk	Teenagers' style of haircut
MP	Military Police

GLOSSARY OF TERMS

OSS	Office of Strategic Services Pathfinder
Pathfinder	Radar equipped lead aircraft
P-51	U.S. fighter aircraft
P-47	U.S. fighter aircraft
P-38	U.S. fighter aircraft
POW	Prisoner of war
QDL	Request a bearing to your station
QDR	Radio Direction Finder Beam
QTF	Altitude and Longitude Position
RAF	British Royal Air Force
Rammkommando	German Kamikaze (suicide) pilot
ROTC	U.S. Reserve Officer Training Corps
Runaway Prop	Engine completely out of control
R & R	Rest & Relaxation
SOS	Emergency call sign, international
SOS	Chipped beef on toast, also known as "shit on a shingle"
Sortie	Mission
Spam	Spiced canned ham
Spitfire	British fighter aircraft
Stalag	German prison camp
Stars and Stripes	U.S. military newspaper in Europe
Sulfa Powder	For infection control
Tail-End Charlie	Last bomber in the low squadron
Typhoon	British fighter aircraft
WAFT	British women in the Air Force
Waist gunner	Left and right interior gunners
Walk-around bottle	Portable oxygen bottle
Wimpy	British bomber
Windmilling	Uncontrollable Propeller
Wheels-down signal	Land your aircraft

For more information about the Mighty Eight and to see additional pictures of the crews and planes, please visit our website www.charlesdhamlin.com or www.fearnoevilbook.com. We would like to thank the Mighty 8th Air Force Historical Society for their cooperation and contribution. For information regarding membership, please call (912) 748-8884 or write to P.O. Box 956 Pooler, GA 31322

9 780615 513652